Still I Stand:

A Life Rewritten

Christopher Angel Machado, M.Ed.

ISBN: 979-8-9936686-1-1

For permissions or inquiries, please contact:

Christopher Angel Machado

✉ christopher.a.machado@gmail.com

Cover and Interior Design by Christopher Angel Machado

Edited by Joseph Collins

✉ info@josephcollinsedits.com

Printed in the United States of America

First Edition, 2025

Published by Machado Mediaworks, LLC

DISCLAIMER

This memoir is a reflection and storytelling of the author's lived experiences, stitched together from memories, emotions, and lessons learned along the way. While every effort has been made to tell this story truthfully, memory is imperfect, and time inevitably reshapes how certain events are remembered. Some names, identifying details, and timelines have been changed or condensed to respect privacy and to honor the spirit of the story rather than the strict chronological order of events.

This is not a work of journalism. It is a work of the heart—an honest attempt by the author to make sense of the moments, the people, and the choices that shaped his life. Wherever possible, the author has strived to extend grace to those who appear in these pages, just as he has worked to extend that same grace to himself.

DEDICATION

To my parents, Maria Frias and Angel Machado:

Not a day goes by that I don't think of you. Everything I do, every milestone I reach, every chapter I write in this life is guided by two unwavering truths: to live the life you were denied the time to finish, and to make you proud with every breath I take. This book is more than my story—it is our story. A tribute to your love, your sacrifices, and your dreams. Your legacy lives on, reborn in my words.

To my students, past, present, and those still to come:

Thank you for being my greatest teachers. You inspire me to be a better educator, a more thoughtful listener, and a more compassionate human every single day. You challenge me, stretch me, and ignite in me a sense of purpose I never knew I needed. You may sit in my classroom, but you live in these pages. This book belongs to you just as much as it belongs to me.

To LGBTQIA+ youth and adults still learning to live out loud:

You are not alone. You are not too much. You are not a phase. You are sacred, whole, and worthy of love exactly as you are. May these pages remind you that truth is not something to fear, it's something to fight for. You deserve stories where you are the hero.

This one is for you.

To survivors of loss, of trauma, of reinvention:

I see you. I am you. This book was born from broken pieces and hard-won healing. If you're still crawling, still crying, still trying—you're still standing. If no one's told you lately: you are not defined by what tried to break you. You are defined by what you built from the ruins.

CONTENTS

Preface
This Is Me

There's the story I let people see—the polished version, edited for public consumption. It came with a smile, a résumé full of gold stars, and a carefully curated image of success on social media. But behind all of that lived another story—one full of questions I was too afraid to ask, truths I wasn't ready to say, and silence that clung to me like armor. This book tells *that* story.

I became a master of the curated self—the overachieving student, the class leader, the "good kid" who never made waves. I smiled when I was supposed to. I excelled when it was expected. I played the role so convincingly, I almost believed it myself. Almost.

But underneath it all was a truth I wasn't ready to face. A quiet ache I couldn't name. A growing sense that no matter how well I followed the script—get good grades, be respectable, go to college, marry the right person, build the perfect life with a white picket fence—it would never truly fit. The lines didn't feel like mine. The future I was told to want didn't feel like home. And so, while everyone applauded the version of me they saw, I quietly carried the weight of the version I kept hidden.

Still I Stand: A Life Rewritten is the story of how I stopped hiding. It's shaped by culture, faith, family, and identity. It's about growing up Dominican and Puerto Rican in a world that demanded I assimilate. About being raised in a Roman Catholic home where queerness was never spoken of—unless in a whisper or a warning. About private schools and public transitions, about being valedictorian in one room and invisible in another. It's about what it means to feel different long before you know why—and the courage it takes to stop running from that difference and lean into it instead.

This memoir isn't linear. Trauma rarely is. Neither is healing.

You'll read about the things that made me—joy and heartbreak, triumph and trauma, friendship and loss. You'll meet the people who shaped me—some with gentle hands, others with sharpened edges.

You'll witness the power of chosen family, the grace of unexpected mentors, and the way even the smallest acts of kindness can reroute a life. And yes, you'll also see the messy, hilarious, sometimes heartbreaking attempts I made to find my place in a world that seemed to have no space carved out for someone like me.

You'll see the many times I failed—publicly, privately, painfully. I've made mistakes. I've stumbled more times than I can count, said the wrong thing, trusted the wrong people, taken the long way when a shortcut was right in front of me.

I've poured my heart into opportunities and relationships that didn't pan out—and into people who didn't deserve it. But no matter how many times I fell, I got back up—scraped, scarred, and still determined. Because that's the thing about growth: it doesn't always look like winning. Sometimes, it looks like surviving failure long enough to discover who you really are.

Along the way, I also learned one of adulthood's hardest truths: not everyone who claps for you wants to see you win. Some of the deepest wounds I carry weren't caused by strangers—they were carved by people I once trusted. Colleagues. Friends. Even family.

You'll read about betrayal, too. About the sting of realizing that not every smile is sincere—and not every ally stays when you start to shine. But every betrayal taught me something. Every setback showed me what I was made of. And through it all, I never stopped believing in the possibility of something better—even when I didn't yet know what that looked like.

I've changed some names and places—not to distance myself from the truth, but to protect the privacy of those whose stories intersect with mine. What remains unfiltered is the emotional honesty. The marrow of this book is mine. These are the words I once buried. These are the pages I never thought I'd write.

This memoir is for anyone who's ever felt the need to shrink themselves to fit someone else's expectations. It's for the kids who sat alone at lunch. For the ones who learned to keep their dreams quiet. For anyone who's ever wondered if their truth was too big, too bold, too much. It's for those still trying to rewrite what they were told about who they are—and what they can be.

Because here's what I've learned: Your truth will wait. It will follow you from state to state, from relationship to relationship, from silence to scream. It will walk with you through every room you enter—quietly, patiently—until the day you're ready to let it breathe.

I was afraid of what would happen when I stopped pretending. What I didn't realize was that the moment I finally said, *This is me,* was the moment I became free. I didn't lose myself—I finally found him. And in telling this story, I continue to find him, again and again.

So yes—*Still I Stand.* Not because the journey was easy. Not because I was fearless. But because, in the end, I chose truth over comfort, growth over safety, and love—real, messy, liberating love—over perfection.

If you're holding this book, maybe you're on that journey too.

I hope these words feel like a friend. I hope they remind you that survival is sacred—and that joy, real joy, waits on the other side of honesty. Most of all, I hope you leave these pages reminded that no matter where you started, no matter how many times you've had to start over, you have the power to rewrite your life.

If you've ever felt like you were too much or not enough... If you've ever walked into a room and scanned for someone who might understand... If you've ever silenced your truth just to survive another day—then I hope these words find you. I hope they remind you: *you are not alone.*

Because despite the chaos, the loss, the pain, and the countless chances I had to stay down... *Still I Stand.* And if I can, so can you.

With a pen and a purpose,

Christopher Angel Machado

Chapter One

Häagen-Dazs and Unsolved Mysteries

My earliest childhood memories begin with the one person who would single-handedly shape my entire life—my hopes, my dreams, and the very reason this book exists: my mother, Maria "Josie" Frias.

Every night before bed, we had a sacred ritual. My mother and I would curl up on the couch and watch *Unsolved Mysteries*, the hauntingly iconic documentary series hosted by Robert Stack. For those unfamiliar, it was an early '90s staple—a montage of real-life mysteries, chilling reenactments of unsolved crimes, missing persons cases, conspiracy theories, and the kind of paranormal tales that could keep a child wide awake long after bedtime. And yet, I never felt afraid. Not when she was by my side.

We'd each enjoy a Häagen-Dazs vanilla milk chocolate ice cream bar—though "share" might be a better word. She always nibbled away the chocolate shell and most of the vanilla, then handed me what was left: the soft, creamy center. That was my favorite part. And maybe, just maybe, she knew that. Maybe it was her way of giving me a little extra sweetness at the end of each day.

That's where my memories with her end.

I didn't know that last night—our final *Unsolved Mysteries*, our final shared ice cream bar—would be *the* last. No warning. No slow fade.

Just... gone. No more bedtime tuck-ins. No more silly songs while brushing my teeth. No warm arms waiting for me after school, no soft voice telling me everything would be okay. She wouldn't see me off to first grade. She wouldn't be there to clap at my high school graduation or beam with pride as I crossed the stage for my bachelor's and, later, my master's degree.

She wouldn't—because she couldn't. She was taken from me in the middle of the night. Rushed to the hospital. And just like that... she never came home.

Maria "Josie" Frias died on January 15, 1995.

She was 34 years old. I was four.

Before she passed, I got to visit her in the hospital. I remember climbing into the narrow bed beside her, not quite understanding what was happening but knowing something wasn't right. She gave me a plush teddy bear dressed in a hospital gown—a small, hopeful gesture meant to soothe a scared little boy. A "get well soon" token.

But she didn't get well.

That bear is still with me. All these years later, I still reach for it when life feels too heavy. There's a comfort in its worn seams, a piece of her that I can still hold. I clutch it when words fail, when grief resurfaces like a wave I thought had already passed. That bear holds more than stuffing—it holds the remnants of her love.

My family says they read books about how to explain death to a child. They say they had difficult conversations with me in the days following her passing. But my memory shields me from them. Trauma has a way of tucking pain into corners we can't reach until we're ready—and I wasn't ready.

What I *do* remember is the funeral.

It was a cold, gray morning—the kind where even the sky seems to mourn. Rain drizzled from the heavens, soaking the earth as if it, too, understood the magnitude of what we'd lost. Everyone wore black, their faces somber, their energy cloaked in sorrow. I, still full of childhood joy, couldn't understand the weight hanging in the air.

No one gave me a straight answer. I remember asking my cousins why everyone looked so sad. They deflected. Distracted. And then... they walked me into the funeral home.

That's when I saw her.

Lying still. Beautiful in her pink lipstick. Too still. Too quiet. A stray hair rested on her lip, and I remember feeling an urge to brush it away—but I didn't. I couldn't. Some small voice inside me knew: *This is the moment everything changes.* I stood frozen, staring at the shell of the woman who once made me laugh with bedtime stories and kissed scraped knees like they were broken bones. In that moment, my innocence was buried alongside her.

As I got older, the questions began to pile up, stacking like unopened letters in the back of my mind. Why did she die so young? Why wasn't I living with my father? Why did my family treat him like an unwelcome ghost?

The answers they gave me were neat. Clean. Sanitized. They said she died of cancer. That before she passed, she had given custody of my brother and me to her sister Julia and her husband, Antonio. And for a time, that was enough—enough to quiet the noise. Enough to let me sleep.

Until it wasn't.

As I grew older, I noticed the tension—the way the air shifted when my father visited. He came on birthdays and Christmas, always with a smile, but never with ease. The adults barely tolerated him. He got different plates, different silverware. They tried to be discreet, but I noticed. Children always do.

Then, one afternoon, I overheard my aunt Julia talking with a friend. The topic of my mother's death came up. Her friend asked, almost too casually, *"He still doesn't know, does he?"* Something inside me snapped awake.

From that moment on, I didn't stop asking questions until someone finally broke. And when they did, the truth spilled out—raw, ugly, real…

My father was a drug addict.

He contracted HIV through intravenous drug use. He unknowingly passed it on to my mother. Her body, weakened from childbirth, couldn't fight it. She died from complications related to HIV/AIDS.

I wasn't ready for that truth.

I wasn't ready to learn that addiction had stolen her from me. That the man I looked up to—the one I'd waited for every holiday—carried the very thing that ended her life.

Suddenly, everything made sense. The scorn in my relatives' eyes. The separate utensils. The resentment that never simmered below the surface—it boiled. To them, he was the villain in a story that ended in tragedy. But to me? He was still my dad.

Broken, yes. Flawed, absolutely. But he was *mine*. And I refused to hate him. Because if the world saw him as unworthy of love, then I would love him twice as hard. Because I was all he had left. And despite his demons, he *never* stopped showing up. When he couldn't get there on his own, someone else made sure he did.

What my dad lacked in stability, he sometimes made up for in the people who loved him. Chief among them was his brother—my uncle Mike. One of the funniest people I've ever known, Uncle Mike didn't just have my dad's back; he practically carried him through life when things got hard. When my dad was homeless, it was Uncle Mike who gave him a roof. When birthdays or holidays came around and my dad said he wanted to see me, it was Uncle Mike who made it happen—not just because my dad didn't have a car (he didn't), but because sometimes he didn't have the courage either. Uncle Mike brought both.

I'm grateful my dad had someone like that in his corner—someone who showed up for him in ways others couldn't or wouldn't. And long after my dad passed, Uncle Mike has continued to show up—

for me. That kind of loyalty, that kind of love, doesn't go unnoticed. It lives in the quiet spaces between grief and gratitude.

As a teenager, I used to pray he would live long enough to see me graduate high school. I begged the universe for that one gift. And in May of 2007, that prayer was answered. My father sat in the audience as I crossed the stage as Senior Class President. He watched his son—*his* son—rise.

Less than a year later, the phone rang. This time, it was Uncle Mike. He told me my father had been hospitalized with pneumonia. It wasn't the first time. With his condition, it had become as routine as the common cold. But something in my uncle's voice made my stomach twist. He handed the phone to my father, and the moment I heard him, I knew.

His voice was faint—like the echo of who he used to be. We talked for a bit, filling the spaces with small talk that mattered more than the words themselves. Before he hung up, he said, *"I love you."* Simple. Final. Like he knew. That night, he suffered a massive brain aneurysm.

I was on the next flight to New York, heart pounding with every mile I crossed. But nothing could have prepared me for what I saw when I walked into that hospital room. He was unrecognizable. Bloated. Motionless. Silent. Hooked up to machines that beeped rhythmically—mocking the absence of life. The doctors were kind but blunt. There was no brain activity. No coming back. It was time to let him go.

When the time came, it was just me and him. No nurses. No doctors. No machines humming to buy us more time. Just a quiet room, fluorescent lights casting shadows on sterile walls, and the unbearable truth settling into my chest like poured concrete. They had disconnected the machines—one by one. And all that remained was him. My father. The man who gave me my name, my quiet comfort, and my fierce eyebrows. The only parent I had left.

I sat by his side, holding his hand like I could somehow anchor him to this world by sheer force of will. His skin was still warm—but it was the kind of warmth that doesn't last. The kind that fades second by second. I watched his chest rise and fall, uneven and fragile—like a wind-up toy winding down for good. I kept whispering, *"It's okay. I'm here. I love you."* But none of it felt okay. None of it ever would.

And then... it happened. His breath staggered. Paused. And then— nothing. No final gasp. No dramatic last word. Just... silence.

I didn't cry. Not at first. I couldn't. I sat there, frozen, staring at the man who used to be my dad slowly becoming a shell. I kept my hand on his chest, as if I could will his heart to keep beating. As if I could trade places. But death doesn't negotiate. It just takes. And in that moment, something broke in me—clean, sharp, and irreparable. Because this wasn't just a man dying. This was my father. My last parent. My only tether to where I came from.

I collapsed into the side of the hospital bed, sobbing like I hadn't since I was a child. My cries weren't poetic or quiet—they were guttural, raw, the kind that comes from a place beyond language. I shook with the weight of it. With the loneliness. With the knowing that there would be no more phone calls, no more visits on holidays or birthdays.

Just absence. Just me.

And if you've never watched someone you love take their last breath—never had to let go while still clinging for dear life—I pray you never have to understand *this* pain. Because in that moment, I didn't just lose my father. It felt like the final page of a chapter had been torn out— no goodbye, no closure, just white space where his voice used to be. And the silence he left behind was deafening.

Angel Machado died on March 31, 2008.

He was 50 years old. I was 18.

For a long time, I didn't tell anyone how they died. Not because I wasn't grieving, but because I was scared. Scared of judgment. Scared of pity. Scared of the stigma wrapped around three little letters: HIV.

In the '90s, HIV/AIDS wasn't just a diagnosis—it was a death sentence laced with shame. People whispered. People assumed. The disease didn't just kill—it erased dignity. There were times I worried people would assume my mother had been a sex worker simply because she died of AIDS. So I stayed quiet.

But silence, I've learned, doesn't protect you. It isolates you. It locks your grief in a box and slaps on a label: *Too messy to unpack*. But I'm unpacking it now.

Years later, I carried their memory in ink. Across my upper back, I had a red ribbon tattooed—bright and defiant—the internationally recognized symbol for HIV/AIDS awareness and support. It's centered between two large angel wings that stretch across my shoulders. On the left wing, in fine black script: *Angel*, my father. On the right: *Maria*, my mother.

Everything but the ribbon was done in black ink—a quiet nod to their passing. But the ribbon? The ribbon blazes in vivid red. Because HIV/AIDS isn't just history. It still lives. Still takes. Still scars.

I chose that spot intentionally—not for aesthetics, but for meaning. It was my way of saying they'd always have my back. That even in death, my parents—my guardian angels—would be right there, looking over my shoulder, watching me move through this world with the strength they left behind.

My parents were more than their illness. More than the stigma. They were real people—flawed, vibrant, loving, complicated. And they deserve to be remembered in the fullness of their humanity.

Speaking my truth isn't about reliving pain. It's about reclaiming power. It's about saying *yes, this happened—and no, it does not define me*. It's about honoring their lives by refusing to let shame write their ending. It's about breaking the silence that stigma built, brick by brick.

I talk about my parents' deaths from HIV/AIDS because they mattered. Because truth matters. Because someone out there might be holding the same story in their heart, too scared to let it breathe. And maybe, if they hear mine, they'll feel less alone. Maybe they'll speak theirs.

This truth doesn't define me—but it shaped me. It taught me empathy. Resilience. The value of honesty, even when it's uncomfortable. *Especially* when it's uncomfortable.

So I speak. For them. For me. For every child who's had to piece together their story from whispers and shadows.

I speak because silence already stole too much from me. And I refuse to let it steal anything else.

Because the truth is—some stories don't start with once upon a time. They start with loss. With absence. With the echo of a door that never closed right and the kind of love that felt borrowed, not promised.

For years, I tried to rewrite my past in the safest way possible—smoothing out the edges, replacing pain with humor, skipping the parts that still made my chest tighten. But the past doesn't like to be edited. It lingers. It waits. And eventually… it finds its way back home. Even to the house that never really felt like one.

Chapter Two

The House That Wasn't Home

After my mother's death, I was sent to live with my maternal aunt and uncle—just as she had wished. I was dropped into a life I didn't choose, surrounded by people I barely knew, in a house that didn't feel like home.

To say I loathed my situation would be the understatement of the century.

My aunt Julia and uncle Antonio were good people—kind, hardworking, and well-meaning—but they were older, traditional, and, at the time, completely foreign to me. They barely spoke English, and I— this skinny, grieving, picky little American boy—was suddenly thrust into their world.

Julia? To five-year-old me, she was insufferable. She ruled her kitchen like a tyrant and expected nothing less than total compliance. Gone were the Kraft Mac & Cheese Deluxe dinners and microwaved Chef Boyardee lunches that brought me small, familiar comforts. In their place: rice, beans, stewed meats, and vegetables I couldn't pronounce— let alone stomach.

I would sit at the table in protest, tears welling in my eyes, my tiny hands clenched around my spoon like it was a weapon in a war I never signed up for. But Julia was unyielding. I wasn't allowed to leave the table until every bite was gone and not a single crumb remained.

Her mission? To fatten me up.

And in that, she succeeded. Within a few years, I transformed from a frail, bony child into what can only be described as a plump little Oompa Loompa. She would beam with pride, unaware of the emotional cost I was quietly paying to survive in this new life.

But there was one saving grace in that household: I inherited a brother and sister. My cousins, Madeline and Roberto, had already grown up under Julia and Antonio's roof. They were older—she was 22, he was 18—they spoke English, and in their presence, I felt seen in a house that often felt like a foreign country.

Roberto, especially, tried to pull me into his world. He was so excited to have a younger "brother" in the house. He imagined backyard games, team sports, and life lessons passed down the way older brothers do. Bless his heart, he tried. He enrolled me in Little League baseball— his grand gesture of brotherhood.

I hated every minute of it.

I loathed the sun beating down on my face, the way the helmet wobbled on my head, how the glove swallowed my tiny hand whole. I hated the dirt under my nails. I hated getting sweaty. I wasn't built for sports—I was built for air conditioning and books, thank you very much.

Still, I gave it one season—long enough to get one hit. Just one. And yet, that single hit was met with such roaring pride you'd think I brought home the World Series trophy. To my family, I was Derek Jeter. Except I never made it to home base. Not literally, not metaphorically. That chapter ended as quickly as it started, and Roberto—poor, sweet Roberto—had to accept a painful truth: I was not his sporty little protégé. I was just… me.

I was a quiet kid. *Too* quiet, they said.

I suppose they thought something must be broken inside me— and who could blame them? I'd lost my mother, been uprooted, stripped of the only world I knew. So they sent me to a child psychologist, hoping he'd crack me open like a piggy bank and pull out the answers. He tried his best, I'm sure. He brought out board games—Monopoly, Connect Four, Sorry—and tried to talk while we played. I let him think he was winning. I played along because I knew how to be the version of me that made adults comfortable.

But deep down? I was drowning.

Eventually, I convinced everyone—including myself—that I didn't need therapy. That I was okay. I wasn't. But I couldn't find the words. And I hated being treated like I was broken. So I did what most hurting children do—I buried it. All of it. And what we bury doesn't disappear. It waits.

Julia and Antonio did the best they could with the hand life dealt them. Raising a five-year-old after your own children are grown isn't just hard—it's asking for a miracle. And somehow, they gave me one anyway. They did it with quiet grace, even when I pushed back.

Julia stayed home and ran the household with military precision, while Antonio worked long hours at the barbershop he owned in downtown Brooklyn. He was the hardest-working man I've ever known. He didn't speak much, but his example spoke volumes. From him, I learned work ethic. I learned that consistency is its own kind of love.

They enrolled me in private Catholic school because they believed it was my best shot at something better. They didn't have to. They weren't obligated. But they honored their promise to my mother. They showed up every day in ways that mattered—especially in the ways I couldn't yet see.

The school they chose was Most Precious Blood School (MPBS), a small Catholic institution tucked into the heart of Brooklyn. With only about 200 students from Pre-K through 8th grade, it felt less like a school and more like an extended family. For a kid quietly unraveling on the inside, MPBS was a lifeline—a place where structure and stability weren't just promised but delivered. About half my teachers were nuns, and while they didn't carry rulers or paddles like the stories my cousins told, they wielded something more effective: a commanding presence and a voice that could silence a room with a single look. Their discipline was sharp— but their care was sharper. In their way, they saw me.

It was there I made my first real friends—the kind who didn't know my whole story but gave me space to just be. I didn't need to explain why I was quiet, or why I sometimes stared out the window like I was searching for something lost. I could just exist. And I met teachers who planted seeds in me that wouldn't bloom for years—but their impact took root all the same.

By the time I reached 8th grade, something remarkable had happened: I had not only adjusted, I had thrived. I finished my time at MPBS as the valedictorian of my graduating class. It was the first time I can remember feeling truly proud of myself—like maybe I was capable of something more.

And it wasn't just about the grades or the speech I gave at graduation. It was proof. Proof that I had survived. That I'd taken everything life had thrown at me—and somehow turned it into a triumph.

The school itself is gone now. Like many Catholic schools in the area, MPBS eventually fell victim to declining enrollment and financial hardship, closing its doors in the late 2000s. But its impact on me lives on.

It gave me structure when my world was chaos. It gave me belonging when home felt like a stranger. And most of all, it gave me a glimpse of what safe could look like—a place where I could breathe, belong, and begin to believe in myself.

And when you're trying to survive the house that wasn't home, sometimes that's all it takes to keep going: to believe there might be something better out there.

In time, I would come to understand what I couldn't grasp as a grieving little boy: Love doesn't always arrive in the package we expect.

Sometimes it shows up as arroz con habichuelas and a stern voice. Sometimes it looks like a man who leaves at dawn and comes home after dark, every single day, without complaint. Sometimes, love means doing what's hard. Especially when it's inconvenient.

And while that house never quite felt like home, it was where I began to understand what resilience really looks like. It's where I started to learn that survival is its own kind of strength—and that sometimes, being loved doesn't feel gentle. But it can still save you.

I slowly acclimated to my new life and made do. I learned to navigate a world that often felt like it wasn't built for me, one quiet moment at a time. But even after I'd accepted the structure of my new normal, the nights still haunted me.

There were so many nights when I would hold that worn teddy bear—my last thread to the world I'd lost—and cry myself to sleep. I'd stare at the ceiling, searching for answers that never came.

Why did she leave me? Why couldn't I go too? The ache of abandonment clung to me like a second skin. I felt so alone. So completely, utterly alone.

But grief has a strange way of blinding us to the people trying their best to love us through it.

Chapter Three

The Hands That Held My Healing

I was lucky—truly lucky—to have grown up in a sprawling, messy, beautiful family filled with cousins, aunts, and uncles who stepped up in ways I'll never be able to repay. They wrapped themselves around me like patchwork armor, offering pieces of my mother back to me through the way they loved. Take Evelyn, for example.

Technically, she's my cousin. But in reality, she's been everything: a mother, a sister, an aunt, a best friend—and sometimes all of those in a single conversation. Whenever she introduced me, she'd say, *"This is my son,"* and I never corrected her. Because that's exactly what she made me feel like.

To say she spoiled me would be an understatement. When I stayed over at her house, we'd play hooky from school and spend the day shopping or eating wherever I wanted. No questions. No hesitation. With her, there was always comfort—a kind of warmth that made the world feel less heavy. Maybe it was because she was so close to my mother. Maybe she recognized the same pain in my eyes that my mom once had. Maybe she just *knew* what I needed without me having to say a word.

To this day, she is my rock—the unwavering constant in a life that's seen more detours than most. And I? I am the son she never had.

Looking back, I realize that healing doesn't arrive all at once. It comes in the form of people who show up when you least expect it. People like Evelyn. People who don't try to replace what you've lost, but who remind you that love still exists—in new, unexpected forms.

I didn't know it then, but those small acts of care—the stolen mornings, the comfort food runs, the laughter in her bed—were slowly stitching together the parts of me I thought had died with my mother. I was still grieving. Still aching. But I was no longer alone. And sometimes, that's enough to keep going.

Evelyn gave me a soft place to land when the world felt sharp and unkind. With her, I learned how to feel joy again—even if it was fleeting. I wasn't healed—not by a long shot. But I had found something steady.

And she wasn't the only steady force standing in the wreckage with me. There was also Ana—Evelyn's mother. My aunt. A woman whose strength wore silk, whose loyalty never asked for attention, and whose love found me quietly, in the places grief had left hollow.

If Julia was the composed heartbeat of the family, Ana was its steady current—graceful on the surface, powerful underneath. She wore elegance with ease, but it was her quiet resilience that defined her. She was a steady light: fierce, loyal, and always ready to rise when her family needed her most. She wears her independence like a badge of honor, and her warmth like an invitation you're lucky to receive.

In her soft, knowing way, Ana understood me in a way words still can't fully capture. She's intuitive—the kind of intuitive that makes you wonder if she's part witch, part guardian angel. She knows when to offer advice without making it feel like a lecture. She knows when I don't need words—just a hug. And when life hit harder than my wallet could handle, she never hesitated. She'd slip me a little extra—no questions asked, no strings attached.

Her generosity was never loud or performative. It was stitched into her very being. And just when life feels too heavy, Ana has an uncanny sense of timing—swooping in with a perfectly timed one-liner or offhand joke that slices through the weight of the moment. Her humor doesn't just make me laugh. It reminds me that survival can be joyful, too.

Even now, as I sit here writing these words, Ana called me to share a dream she had: In it, I was a young child again, running toward her, gleaming with excitement, shouting, *"I saw her! I saw my mom. She's okay!"* She had no idea I was deep into writing this memoir—unearthing old grief, honoring old love, stitching together every broken memory.

Her dream wasn't just a coincidence. It was a soft knock on the door of my soul, a whisper from the universe meant just for me. As I sifted through wounds and memories, it felt like a hand reaching across dimensions—reminding me that love doesn't vanish with time or distance.

My mother's love. Ana's love. They're stitched into the fabric of who I am, woven so deeply that even in the quiet spaces—even in the ache of missing them—they find ways to reach me. Their presence isn't confined to the past. It *breathes* with me. *Walks* with me. *Writes* with me.

And maybe that's what the dream was really trying to tell me: That even as I wade through grief and memory, I am *never* walking alone.

In a story built on loss, survival, and becoming, moments like that remind me of a few things: Some hands don't just hold you—they *heal* you. Some love doesn't just stay—it *carries* you forward. And some people—like Ana—are proof that family isn't defined by blood, but by the way someone shows up when the world tries to knock you down.

But Ana wasn't the only one who wrapped me in that kind of love. There were others, woven into the fabric of my childhood—the ones who didn't just share my bloodline but who shaped my sense of home in ways words can barely capture. Among them are my cousins— Annie and Sandy. But calling them "cousins" doesn't quite cut it. They've always felt more like sisters—the kind you don't choose but somehow end up needing more than you ever realized. I grew up with them. Weekends in my aunt's backyard, running wild, or curled up on the couch watching movies we probably weren't old enough to watch.

Annie and I were born on the same exact day and year—and yes, *I'm* the older one. Don't let her tell you otherwise. She's my twin flame in every sense: the yin to my yang, the soft lullaby to my chaotic karaoke. Annie is quiet, thoughtful, and emotionally attuned, while I tend to be the loudest laugh in the room and the last one to leave the party *(I get that from my mom)*. Now, she's a mother of three—and honestly, I don't know how she does it. I can barely keep a houseplant alive without a pep talk and a YouTube tutorial.

But even as life gets busier and messier, our bond never wavers. She knows when to offer comfort, when to offer space, and when to simply show up. There's an unspoken understanding between us that doesn't need grand gestures—it's stitched into our shared history, in the way we know each other's hearts without ever needing to explain a thing.

And then there's Sandy. If Annie is the whisper, Sandy is the megaphone. She's got a sense of humor that's both dark and absolutely lethal, paired with a personality I can only describe as a *weapon of mass destruction*—especially if you cross her. In fact, she doesn't just give the silent treatment—she invented it. She's not the type to coddle. "I love you" isn't in her regular vocabulary. But her love language is a unique mix of medical check-ins and tough-love text messages:

> *"Did you drink water today?"*
>
> *"Don't forget to take your vitamins."*
>
> *"When was the last time you saw your doctor?"*
>
> *"Get off your ass and go to the gym."*

And strangely enough… *that's* how you know she cares.

Now, Sandy's a mother of two—an actual miracle come to life if you know her personality. The fact that she grew two tiny humans inside that chaos-core body of hers and somehow became a fiercely devoted mom? Iconic. Her kids may not always get lullabies, but they'll grow up with backbone, humor, and a mom who doesn't just protect—she *prepares*.

They both helped shape my childhood into something joyful and safe. And now, as adults, they continue to do what they've always done—keep me grounded, call me out when needed, and remind me that home isn't always a place. Sometimes, it's two loud, loving, wildly different women who've known you since your baby teeth were falling out—and love you just the same, crooked smile and all.

What I didn't realize back then was that grief never really leaves you. It just shapeshifts. It hides in quiet moments, lingers in the corners of your laughter, and eventually demands to be dealt with—whether you're ready or not.

Julia and Antonio's house was where I lived. But Evelyn's arms? That was the first place that ever felt like home after my mother died. And maybe that's the truth of it all: I had to survive the house that wasn't home in order to recognize the ones that were. The ones found in Evelyn's embrace. In Annie's gentle loyalty. In Sandy's loud, protective love. The kind of homes you don't move into—you grow into, one memory at a time.

But not every part of my childhood felt like home. Some parts felt like weather—unpredictable, loud, and capable of leaving a mark. That's where my brother, Junior, comes in.

His real name is William, but everyone called him Junior. We were close growing up, connected by a shared love of cars. We'd spend hours flipping through auto magazines, naming our dream rides like we were building futures in chrome and horsepower. He liked the loud ones, the flashy ones. I preferred clean lines and power under the hood. Still, it was *our thing*. In a world where so much felt uncertain, cars gave us common ground. Something to dream about. Something that made sense.

Our bond wasn't built on softness—it was built on survival.

After my mother passed, the world we knew shattered. We were split apart. He went to live with his father. I stayed behind in a different home, with a different life. We ended up in different schools, different neighborhoods, different worlds. And the distance between us wasn't just physical—it grew with time, with silence, with pain we didn't have words for yet.

Eventually, Junior dropped out of school. And while I didn't know how to save him from that choice, I carried it with me. His story—the way it veered off-course—lit something in me I couldn't ignore. You'll read more about that later. How his journey, even in its detours, became fuel for my own.

Junior is now the proud father of two wonderful children—Haley and Junior. And although life hasn't always treated him fairly, my brother shows up. He works hard. He provides. He pours into his kids with the kind of love and determination that makes you stop and take note. I aspire to be the kind of father he is one day—unwavering, devoted, full of heart.

He didn't know it then, but he was one of my first reasons. One of my earliest *whys*. That why would carry me through moments when everything else fell apart—moments that would mark the end of who I was, and the beginning of who I was becoming.

But no journey worth writing about is made alone. There were people—quiet constants—who stayed behind the scenes, holding me up when life tried to knock me down. People like Sandra.

Sandra wasn't born into my family, but somehow, she became part of it in all the ways that mattered. She and Madeline had met back in the fourth grade—two girls thrown together by a twist of fate who grew into lifelong friends. Their bond eventually extended to their parents, who became close with Julia and Antonio. So close, in fact, that when Sandra's family needed a new place to live, Julia and Antonio offered them the vacant upstairs apartment in our building.

It started as convenience. It became something much deeper. Sandra was older than me, but she never treated me like an annoying little kid who hung around too much. Over time, she became more than just a neighbor. More than just a babysitter. She became the sister I chose for myself—the one who stepped into my life not because she had to, but because she *wanted* to.

Madeline was the sister life handed me first—and I love her for it. But Sandra? She was the sister I found. The one my heart picked out all on its own. She was there through it all—the birthdays, the heartbreaks, the small victories no one else noticed but meant the world to me.

When I turned 21, there was no question who I wanted by my side: it was Sandra. She wasn't just part of my childhood; she became part of every milestone that followed. Even now, she's one of the first people I call—whether I'm celebrating a new chapter, falling for someone new, or unraveling during one of life's many existential crises.

She listens without judgment. She advises without preaching. She loves without conditions. With Sandra, I am always seen. I am always heard. I am always safe.

She may not have been written into the opening pages of my life story, but somewhere along the way, she became one of its most important characters. And though she's often been in the background—quiet, steady, loyal—her love has been anything but small.

If I've built a life worth being proud of, it's because people like Sandra stood quietly behind me, holding up the parts of me I didn't even know were breaking. Without her, I might've made it—but it wouldn't have been with nearly as much hope, or nearly as much heart.

When I look back now, I realize it wasn't the easy days that shaped me. It was the losses. The quiet victories. The people who stayed. The people who didn't. It was the breaking. The building. The long, messy *becoming* of someone who refused to stay small.

And as I stood at the edge of everything I thought I knew, life was already preparing to test me in ways I could never have imagined. It was about to break my body. And in doing so, it would force me to find the fight that had been inside me all along.

Chapter Four

The Day My Body Broke and My Becoming Began

The summer I turned eleven, my body declared war on me.

One morning, I woke up with unbearable stomach pain—the kind that makes you think you're dying. I must've taken six showers that day, the hot water the only thing that offered even the slightest relief. But no amount of water or over-the-counter meds could touch what was happening inside me. When nothing worked, Julia rushed me to the ER at Lutheran Medical Center in Brooklyn (now NYU Langone Hospital) and called the rest of the family.

What I didn't know then was that most of my cousins were upstate at the Woodbury Common Premium Outlets with Evelyn for her birthday—her favorite way to celebrate. They had just sat down at an Applebee's when Julia's call came through. According to them, they didn't even think twice. They packed up, piled into the car, and sped back to Brooklyn like an emergency response team on a mission.

By the time they arrived, my fever had spiked to nearly 106°F. I was drenched in sweat and surrounded by bags of ice, with a hospital team trying everything to bring my temperature down. The culprit? An inflamed and infected appendix. The infection was spreading, but they couldn't operate with my fever so dangerously high. So they monitored me, wrapped me in ice packs, and administered Tylenol suppositories (not exactly a highlight of my childhood, let's just say).

Once my fever stabilized, they prepped me for surgery. But as they wheeled me toward the operating room, I felt it happen—my appendix burst. I don't know what it feels like to get shot, but in that moment, I imagine it comes pretty close. The pain was so overwhelming, it knocked me out cold.

When I came to, I was in the ICU. Julia was beside me, her eyes heavy with worry. I had a tube threaded up my nose and down into my stomach to drain the infection. Sounds fun, right? Not when you've just had your tonsils and adenoids removed two weeks earlier. My throat was still raw, and that tube was the final straw. So, I did what any self-respecting eleven-year-old would do—I yanked it out. Julia panicked and ran to grab a nurse, but the damage was already done. And honestly? I felt better.

My family didn't just *arrive*—they took over. One or two at a time at first, like a slow, steady tide… But then the tide rose, and suddenly the waiting room looked less like a hospital and more like a family reunion in crisis. Aunts in heels clicking against the tile floor. Uncles arguing with nurses at the front desk. Cousins clutching coffee cups and crumpled fast-food wrappers after the long drive back from upstate. There were tears. There were prayers. And far too many opinions about which doctor should be consulted.

And somehow, even in all the chaos, there was comfort.

People came from every corner of my family tree—some I hadn't seen in months, others who booked last-minute flights from Florida the moment they heard I was in the ICU. They filled every seat, leaned against every wall, and turned that sterile emergency room into a war room. They brought snacks, blankets, stories, and the kind of emotional support that only comes from a family that's been through hell—and refuses to let anyone go through it alone.

While I was unconscious, they waited. While doctors monitored my vitals, they monitored each other. And when visiting hours finally opened, they came in like a wave—quietly, respectfully, but fully present. They took turns by my bedside. Squeezing my hand. Brushing hair from my forehead. Whispering things like, *"You scared the hell out of us."*

And they didn't leave. Not for sleep. Not for food. Not until they knew I was going to be okay.

Just when I thought my dignity had officially left the building, life had one more humbling moment in store.

Enter Lisa: Evelyn's sister, another honorary sibling, and someone who's been cleaning up after me longer than I care to admit. This wasn't our first encounter with bodily functions and questionable life choices. Years earlier—when I was a stubborn toddler with no sense of aim—I peed all over her while she was trying to change me. No warning. No mercy. Just pure toddler betrayal.

And now, decades later, there we were again: me in a hospital gown, her with that same exasperated expression, applying hydrocortisone cream to my ass like it was just another Tuesday.

She did it with an eye roll, a crack of a joke, and a tenderness that somehow made the whole thing feel a little less humiliating.

If you're cringing—good. So was I. But the truth is, the real story doesn't live in the comfortable moments.

Because that's what real love looks like sometimes—not grand speeches or dramatic gestures, but the people who stay. The ones who laugh with you through the worst of it. The ones who hold your dignity when you're too broken to hold it yourself.

In that moment—fevered, stitched, and surrounded—I understood something that would echo throughout my life: I wasn't alone. I never had been. Even when the world felt fractured or uncertain, my family showed up—arms full of love and chaos. And as you'll come to see… they always did. They always do.

Somewhere in the background, usually armed with a sarcastic comment and a bottle of hand sanitizer, was Nancy—Evelyn and Lisa's sister. An educator like me. And one of the few people who could still make me laugh when laughing felt impossible. She calls me *"Mr. VIP,"* partly because I somehow turned my hospital room into a full-blown family reunion, and partly because, in her words: *"Seriously, Chris… only you could almost die and still expect first-class service."*

She wasn't wrong.

With Nancy, there's always laughter tucked into the corners of even the worst days. She reminds me—without ever saying it—that survival isn't just about medicine or miracles. Sometimes, it's about the people who stay. The ones who make sure that even without your mother's arms around you, you still feel held.

And maybe that's the thing about being shaped by loss and separation—it sharpens your vision.

It teaches you what absence feels like... so you can recognize presence when it shows up. Sometimes in the form of a crowded emergency room. Sometimes in a cousin's quiet loyalty. It helps you define the kind of life you want to build, the kind of love you want to give, and the kind of leader you choose to become.

Because when that chapter of my life closed—stitched together with grief, resilience, and the arms of those who refused to let me go numb—I made a choice:

I wasn't going to disappear into silence.

I was going to speak.

I was going to show up.

I was going to run.

And I did.

What came next? Let's just say... the quiet kid in the corner didn't stay there for long.

Chapter Five

From Wallflower to Class President

There were parts of me I learned to hide—even in the safest places. Even with Evelyn. Even surrounded by family who loved me. There was a silence I carried inside—a quiet ache I couldn't name yet. Love was present, yes, but so was fear. Not the kind that creeps in from dark corners, but the kind that lives in your chest, whispering that if you ever spoke your truth aloud, everything you'd found—every person, every sliver of comfort— might vanish.

The house I lived in taught me many things: how to be strong, how to be grateful, how to survive.

But it didn't teach me how to be myself. Toward the tail end of middle school, my family made the decision to move to Florida. My uncle Antonio was retiring after forty years as a barber, and I was on the cusp of high school, so the timing made sense. A fresh start, they said. A better life, they hoped. And while the idea had its glimmers of excitement, I wrestled with the weight of leaving behind the life I'd only just begun to settle into— friends I'd finally grown close to, cousins who felt more like siblings, and a familiar rhythm that had started to feel... safe.

I remember that flight from New York to Florida in the summer of 2003—the one that made the move permanent. I don't remember crying that much in a long time. It felt like grieving all over again, but this time, it was a different kind of loss. I wasn't just leaving a city—I was being pulled away from the first version of "home" I'd stitched together out of grief and love. And somewhere deep in that grief was a fear I couldn't yet name: that starting over would mean burying even more pieces of myself. That I'd have to hide even deeper behind the mask I'd already grown used to wearing.

What no one knew at the time—what I barely understood myself—was that the hardest part about moving wasn't the packing, or the goodbyes, or even the uncertainty of starting high school in a strange new place. It was the truth I was still trying to outrun. The truth that would follow me from one zip code to another, quietly waiting for the day I'd be brave enough to set it free.

During the transition from New York to Florida, I first lived with my sister Madeline and her family. They were the first to find a house and settle in. Six months later, Julia and Antonio found a home of their own. I'll never forget the day we pulled into the driveway with the realtors. The sun cast this warm, golden hue over the roof, and something inside me just knew—this was it. This was the one. After months of visiting cold, empty houses that felt more like shells than shelter, this house *felt* different. It felt like possibility. Like safety. Like the beginning of something new.

It was tucked inside a quiet, gated community made up of nine subdivisions, complete with a clubhouse, fitness center, swimming pools, and sports courts. The lawns were perfectly trimmed. The trees stood tall like guardians. Kids rode their bikes along the sidewalks without a care in the world. And for the first time in what felt like forever, I could picture a life here—one where laughter echoed in the hallways and dinner wasn't just about food, but about togetherness. It didn't just look like a home. It felt like one.

That summer, my sister had done her homework and researched high schools that would be a good fit for me. Since I'd graduated 8th grade as Valedictorian, I had several options. One of them was Fort Lauderdale High School's Pre-Law and Public Affairs Magnet Program. At the time, I was genuinely interested in becoming a lawyer—or working in politics, particularly International Affairs, like one of my cousins. But there was one major deterrent: the commute. Fort Lauderdale High School was 18 miles away—roughly a 45-minute ride. To make it work, I'd have to wake up around 4:00 a.m. every morning just to catch the bus. And that just wasn't in the cards for me.

The more reasonable—and let's be honest, more exciting—option was the brand-new high school opening in our neighborhood: Monarch High School.

Coconut Creek, nestled in Broward County, is part of South Florida's Fort Lauderdale metro area, sitting about 37 miles north of Miami. It proudly calls itself the *Butterfly Capital of the World*, thanks to Butterfly World—the largest butterfly aviary on Earth, home to over 20,000 butterflies.

Sounds magical, right? Until you realize the only butterflies I ever saw in Coconut Creek were printed on brochures or slapped onto gas station keychains. Still, that's how the school got its name: Monarch

High. Home of the Knights. Because nothing says *medieval warrior* like a gentle pollinator.

While I was excited to start fresh in the Sunshine State, the thought of going to a massive public school—without knowing a single soul—was absolutely terrifying. Coming from a private Catholic school with just 200 students hadn't exactly prepared me for the social hurricane of a campus with nearly 2,400.

The first person I met at Monarch was Ms. Lucas—now Mrs. Murray—and to this day, I truly believe the universe planted her in my life on purpose. She radiated calm. She had this warm, grounding energy that made the chaotic buzz of a high school office feel strangely safe. One look, and I swear she could see straight into my soul—like she already knew what I'd been through, even before I said a word.

She didn't toss around motivational quotes or deliver dramatic pep talks. She simply *showed up*—kind, steady, and real. And in those early days, when everything felt foreign and overwhelming, she gave me exactly what I needed most: reassurance. Her presence made the halls less intimidating. She loosened the knot in my chest just enough for me to breathe. She wasn't just a guidance counselor. She was my anchor.

So when school started that fall, I did what felt safe. Every morning after the bus dropped me off, I'd head straight to Ms. Lucas' office— whether she was there or not—and sit quietly until class started. The cafeteria, with its loud laughter and clattering trays, was a full-on sensory nightmare. But her office? That was my sanctuary. When she was in, we'd chat about school, life, and everything in between. She never judged. She just *listened.* I kept that routine going for nearly two years—like clockwork.

Eventually, she gently nudged me out of my shell. She encouraged me to join clubs and try extracurriculars—not just to make friends, but to build a college résumé and open doors to scholarships.

The idea of voluntarily joining anything felt like social suicide. But Ms. Lucas knew exactly how to ease me in.

She was the advisor for SADD—Students Against Destructive Decisions. Originally launched as *Students Against Drunk Driving,* the group had expanded its mission in the late '90s to address broader issues: drug use, violence, suicide, and risky behavior. It turned out to be the perfect space for me. A way to use my own life experiences to support others—while still keeping one foot firmly in my comfort zone. By sophomore year, I even ran for a leadership position—and became the club's treasurer.

Was it scary? Absolutely. Did I stumble? Many times. But something unexpected happened: I started to bloom. I went from the nervous kid hiding out in a guidance counselor's office to someone slowly building a voice. And Ms. Lucas saw it before I did.

I'll never forget the day she looked at me and said: *"Chris, I love having you here… but it's time. You can't spend your high school years hiding in this office. You need to go out there and make some friends."* That conversation stuck with me.

Now, let me pause and give you a little context. I grew up in a Dominican household where planning parties isn't just part of our culture—it's practically a sacred art form. I also came of age watching movies like *10 Things I Hate About You*, *She's All That*, *Napoleon Dynamite*, and of course, *Mean Girls*. You know what they all have in common? Iconic, unforgettable prom scenes.

And that's when I had my lightbulb moment: I didn't just want to go to prom. I wanted to plan it. But pulling that off would require something I didn't yet have: Friends. Influence. Power. I needed to get elected Class President. Which meant I had to do the unthinkable: I had to become... popular. *(Cue Galinda's "Popular" from Wicked—jazz hands and all.)*

I told Ms. Lucas about my plan. She blinked a few times—probably processing the whiplash of my sudden ambition—but then she smiled. She didn't laugh. She didn't doubt. She simply laid out the steps I needed to take.

Step one: Show up. I walked into my first class meeting and was greeted by a sea of girls who looked at me like I'd just stumbled into the sacred circle of their coven uninvited. Without skipping a beat, I introduced myself and said: *"Hi, my name is Christopher Machado, and I'm going to be your next Class President."*

Let's just say... they were not thrilled. Who did I think I was? A boy waltzing in like a Disney prince, making proclamations. I could practically feel the eye-rolls ricocheting around the room.

So, I pivoted. I slowed down. I got to know them individually. I listened. I learned. I earned their trust—not by demanding it, but by showing up with humility (and, yes, maybe a few well-placed compliments and snacks).

Next mountain: becoming well-known across campus. Fortunately, I had a secret weapon: I ran the school's morning announcements. My face was broadcast across classrooms every morning, which helped make me a familiar presence. I became "that guy"—the smart one, the funny one, the "oh yeah, I know him" guy.

That year, I won the election. I became Junior Class President. I made promises, delivered results, and raised over $10,000 in one year. That success didn't just give me credibility—it gave me momentum. By senior year, when it was time to run again, my opponent never stood a chance.

Becoming Senior Class President wasn't just a win. It was a declaration. It marked the journey—from the scared, silent kid hiding in a counselor's office... to the confident, driven young man leading his class. It was proof that I could walk into a room, claim space, and be chosen. I had found my voice.

And even if no one knew the whole truth yet—not even me—I was finally starting to believe I had the power to write my own script.

Chapter Six

Blockbuster and Blue Eyes

I didn't have the language for it then, but I always felt like I was orbiting something I couldn't name. While other kids moved through life on a familiar track—crushes, dances, awkward flirtations that made sense— I was stuck in a loop of confusion and curiosity. There was something about me that didn't quite click with the world I was growing up in. Not wrong, exactly... just off-script.

In Catholic school, difference wasn't something you explored—it was something you prayed away. So I learned early how to blend in. Smile at the right moments. Compliment the right girls. Laugh when expected. But deep down, I was performing. Behind the performance was a boy quietly wondering why he couldn't stop staring at the covers of *Men's Health* magazines in checkout lines, or why he kept "accidentally" rewinding certain movie scenes a few too many times.

There was a script I was supposed to follow, but the lines never quite fit. I played the part, but there was always this quiet dissonance humming beneath it all—like background static in a room full of applause.

From as early as I can remember, I knew which girls were pretty—but I felt a curiosity toward guys. I'd always pick the prettiest girl and try to catch her attention with a handwritten note in class (you know the ones—*Check yes or no if you like me too*). Spoiler alert: it never worked. Pitiful, nostalgic, and absolutely tragic.

Years later, after trying too hard to date girls, I would finally understand there's a very real difference between recognizing someone is attractive and actually being attracted to them. I found myself leaning into that feeling in quiet, coded ways—lingering too long in the men's underwear aisle, replaying sensual movie scenes (and it definitely wasn't for the women).

Blockbuster—yes, I'm officially dating myself—became a kind of sanctuary, especially during those pubescent high school years when I discovered the International Film section left a lot less to the imagination than the American one. Who knew French cinema would give teenage me a full-blown sexual awakening?

Still, I didn't act on any of those urges—not until senior year. Not until I met *him*.

At that point, I was knee-deep in extracurriculars and campus leadership. I was the student voice in every space that needed one: PTA meetings, Open House, Family Nights—you name it. If there was a clipboard, a mic, or a photo op, I was there.

It was during one of those events that I met the mother of the guy who would change everything. She and I connected almost instantly. In retrospect, I think it was her gentle, maternal energy—something I always gravitated toward. In nearly every conversation, she brought him up. *"You have to meet my son,"* she'd say. *"He'd love you. You two would be such good friends."*

Little did *she* know. Little did *we* know.

Our first interaction was over the phone. I was talking to her when she suddenly passed it to him. I heard his voice—and instantly, I was grinning like an idiot. There was excitement in his tone, this new kid chatting with the older, now-popular guy at school. It felt like a scene straight out of a teen movie, and I was all in.

The best part? He lived in my neighborhood. Just one subdivision over.

From that moment on, we were inseparable. We texted nonstop. He became the first person I talked to in the morning and the last one I messaged at night. And when we finally met in person... I fell. Instantly. Hard. His ocean-blue eyes melted me like a snowman in Florida.

At first, our conversations were layered with innuendos and coded language—but underneath it all, we both knew exactly what we were saying.

And then came our first kiss.

The setting? An empty construction site during my lunch break from my first job at Walgreens. Because nothing says "young love" like piles of insulation and steel beams. Nicholas Sparks could *never*. What started as a dare turned into a moment I'll never forget—an exhilarating, life-changing kiss that knocked the breath right out of me.

In that moment, I knew. This felt right. I like guys. And there was no turning back.

Our "relationship" was short-lived—a whirlwind that came and went faster than I could process. But while it lasted, he was everything. For the first time, I felt seen. I felt heard. I felt loved—or at least what I thought love was. Maybe it was lust, or maybe just the thrill of finally being chosen. Either way, he made me feel something I'd never felt before. Something electric. Something real.

Unfortunately, teenage boys aren't exactly known for their communication skills. And when Homecoming rolled around—the night I'd been quietly dreaming about—it all unraveled.

I wanted him to be my date. Or at least ride in the limo with me as my "friend." We both knew it meant more than that. But that's not what happened.

His mom had called me earlier that day, asking when I'd be ready and how I was getting to the venue. But I was in West Palm Beach with my family, caught up in plans I had no control over. I gave her the best answer I could, assuming we'd figure it out later. But when I tried reaching out—texts, calls, anything—I was met with silence. Left on read. Ignored. And just like that, something shifted.

What could've been resolved with a simple conversation turned into a deafening, soul-crushing silence. He ghosted me. The entire night.

Imagine standing in a crowded room—music blaring, lights flashing, everyone dancing—and still feeling completely alone. That's what it felt like. I watched the boy I was falling for from across the room while he acted like I didn't exist. It wrecked me.

The pain was sharp and familiar—but this time, it cut deeper. Because I had let him in. I had trusted him. And he couldn't even look at me. In the days and weeks that followed, I tried everything I could to talk to him, to understand what had happened. But he avoided me like the plague. I knew his schedule, his routine, his favorite hallway shortcuts—but he rerouted his life like I was a hazard to avoid. He surrounded himself with people so thick I couldn't get near him without looking desperate. And I couldn't risk that. No one knew my secret. I still had a reputation to protect—and a version of myself I was trying hard to perform.

As a last-ditch effort, I convinced one of the front office secretaries—a kind woman I called my "school mom"—to call him out of class under some made-up excuse. *He can't escape me now,* I thought. *He has to talk to me.*

But the second he laid eyes on me, I knew. The look on his face said everything. Ice-cold. Distant. Like I had somehow betrayed him. Without saying a word, he turned and walked back toward class.

I followed him.

In a quiet stairwell, with no one around, I grabbed his arm. I needed him to hear me. I needed closure. I needed *something.*

"I love you," I said, tears in my eyes, heart in my throat.

He looked at me—for what felt like an eternity—with those ocean- blue eyes and said simply, *"I need to go back to class."*

And just like that, my world shattered. He didn't want me. And I didn't know why.

Maybe he'd found someone else. Maybe he'd lost interest. Maybe I'd done something wrong. I combed through our texts, replayed every conversation, studied his social media for clues. I came up empty— except for one haunting detail: his MySpace profile song.

Remember MySpace? Everyone had that one song that auto-played when you visited their page—equal parts dramatic and deeply personal. His was "How to Save a Life" by The Fray. The lyrics echoed a kind of regret and confusion that mirrored my own: *Where did I go wrong? I lost a friend.* I listened to it on repeat, hoping it would give me answers. It didn't.

But it did give me a soundtrack to my heartbreak.

Eventually, the pain softened, but it never fully disappeared. So I did what I'd always done—I redirected the ache. I threw myself into academics, extracurriculars, and the task at hand. After all, I still had a prom to plan. I focused on success as a form of distraction—and maybe, just maybe, as a quiet form of revenge. It was my first real lesson in the phrase: *The best revenge is a life well lived.*

I went off to college. Life moved forward. And somewhere along the way, we reconnected—briefly—during one of my visits home. But the spark had faded. Whatever we'd had back then didn't survive the distance. We never talked about why it ended. We just let the past be the past. *(Cue "Water Under the Bridge" by Adele.)*

We drifted into separate lives, orbiting each other through the distant window of social media. But recently, we hung out again—just as friends—while he was visiting family in town. We drank, we laughed, we reminisced. And at one point, I caught myself staring into those same ocean-blue eyes, still amazed at how he somehow looked even better than he did back then.

But this time, something had changed.

This time, I made a conscious choice: to leave the memory of us exactly where it belonged—in the past. Because he's happily married now. To a man. With a thriving military career and a life he's built with intention and pride. I wasn't going to disturb that. I didn't want to.

And the truth is… I didn't need to.

Because that first love—complicated, short-lived, and heart-wrenching—taught me something that shaped every relationship that followed. It taught me that love, especially your first, is rarely neat or easy. It's messy. Consuming. It doesn't always last, but it always leaves a mark. It showed me the high of being truly seen and the devastation of being suddenly unseen. It gave me my first taste of heartbreak and, with it, my first real glimpse of who I was and what I needed.

But most importantly, it prepared me for what came next.

Because when you've loved in silence—when you've carried the weight of your truth in secret—you eventually reach a crossroads. You either shrink to survive… or you step into the light.

And I was tired of shrinking.

Coming out wasn't easy. But loving him—and losing him—gave me the strength to even consider it. That loss didn't break me. It built the courage to finally stop lying to myself.

Chapter Seven

Father, Son, and the Holy Shit I'm Gay

I wasn't out in high school—but there were clues.

Most of my closest friends were girls, giving me a front-row seat to every whispered crush, messy breakup, and juicy piece of gossip. But when it came to boys, I felt like I was playing a role I never auditioned for. While my classmates obsessed over first kisses and hallway hand-holding, I deflected questions about who I liked with recycled lines like, *"I'm just focused on school right now."*

I wasn't "flamboyant," but I definitely wasn't whatever version of "masculine" teenage boys were busy performing. While they debated tux rentals and post-prom parties, I was in the student government office fighting tooth and nail over chair sashes and floral arrangements like my GPA depended on it.

Let's just say... subtlety was not my strong suit.

And while they compared bench press numbers and body counts, I was far more invested in decoding why Regina George wore army pants and flip flops. Being closeted felt like starring in a play where everyone else had the script but me. Every day was a mental gymnastics routine—how to answer without giving away too much, how to sound interested in girls without sounding too interested, how to laugh at jokes that made my skin crawl.

I was always on—hyper-aware of my voice, my posture, my laugh. Was I standing too close to him? Was that hand gesture too much? Did my eye roll read as "sassy" or just annoyed?

I could recite straight-boy small talk like a second language, but I never felt fluent. I was fluent in code-switching, fluent in charm, fluent in being everything to everyone—except honest with myself.

There were moments—small, charged ones—when I could tell people suspected. A lingering glance. A knowing smirk. An "innocent" question dropped like bait: *Are you sure you're not into guys?* But no one asked me outright. Not at school. I held too much influence, and they knew it.

I wasn't just a student—I was a brand. Friends with teachers, chummy with admin, keeper of everyone's secrets. If I wanted to, I could ruin someone's social life before third period. So they kept their suspicions to themselves. I wasn't gossip fodder—I was a liability.

Some were curious.

Some were cruel.

Most stayed quiet.

There were teachers who looked at me a little too long, with a strange mix of affection and caution. Friends who'd say things like *"You're basically one of the girls,"* thinking it was a compliment. Guys who called me *"sus"* behind my back but still slid me their homework. I became a master at being in on the joke and the punchline.

But silence builds pressure. And eventually, the closet starts to feel more like a coffin.

Coming out wasn't just about saying *I'm gay*. It was about letting go of the version of myself I'd spent years curating. It meant risking friendships, invitations, comfort—maybe even safety. It meant telling the truth when the lie had become second nature.

Before I told a soul, I rehearsed reactions like flashcards: *Would she still invite me to sleepovers? Would he still dap me up in the hallway? Would the teachers look at me differently? Would my family…?*

Yeah. That last one? I avoided it for as long as I could.

But I knew the truth wasn't going to stay quiet forever. You can only keep the walls from closing in for so long.

Brenna was the first person I ever told—and honestly, I couldn't have picked a better accomplice. She's a redheaded firecracker with a heart of gold and a mouth that refuses to whisper. Subtlety isn't her ministry. She has this rare gift of making you feel completely safe and slightly terrified at the same time—like she'd fight someone for you in a parking lot, then bake them cookies afterward to make peace.

It happened one afternoon as she was driving me home from school in her prized possession: a 2005 black Toyota Corolla Sport. That car was her baby, and you'd better believe she treated it like it had VIP status in every parking lot. When I told her I was gay, she didn't flinch. She just looked at me, tilted her head like I'd said I preferred Coke over Pepsi, and replied, *"Well, duh."* Classic Brenna—equal parts sass, warmth, and unwavering loyalty. If I had to come out all over again, I'd still choose her to be the first to know.

We're still best friends, 22 years later—proof that some soul connections are simply built to last. She's still the person I call when I need advice, when life feels a little too heavy, or when I need someone to talk me off the ledge because a guy I like left me on read or used a period instead of an exclamation point in a text. It's no coincidence that Brenna became a psychotherapist—she's been diagnosing my nonsense since high school. And trust me, she's really good at her job, even if she still delivers unsolicited TED Talks in the group chat.

These days, she's a loving wife, a model mother to three beautiful girls, and somehow, an even better friend than she was back then.

It's important to me that I mention her in this story—not just because she was the first person I ever told the truth to, but because she met that truth with love, zero hesitation, and a loyalty that never wavered. She reminded me that I could be fully seen and still fully accepted. And for someone who had spent so long hiding, that moment was everything.

But here's the thing about coming out—once you crack the door open, you hope people will knock before barging in. That they'll wait until you're ready, until you feel safe. Unfortunately, not everyone honors that kind of boundary. Especially not family.

Not long after I came out to Brenna, the truth found its way into the wrong hands—without my permission, and without my voice.

Roberto, my cousin—who, by all intents and purposes, had become like a brother to me—outed me to Julia and Antonio after going through my phone. I don't know if it was carelessness, spite, or some misguided attempt at "help," but one thing was certain: it wasn't his story to tell. And it definitely wasn't his to weaponize.

The conversation that followed was everything I had feared and more. They didn't yell. They didn't scream. They didn't kick me out. But in some ways, what they did was worse. They reduced me. Not to a sinner. Not to a mistake. But to a broken thing in need of fixing.

Julia sat me down and asked the question again and again, like repetition might summon a different answer.

"Are you gay?"

"No."

"Are you gay?"

"No."

"Are you gay?"

...

Eventually, I broke.

I told her I wasn't gay—I was bisexual. It wasn't a lie, not entirely. The truth is, I was still trying to figure it out myself. I said I still wanted to get married in a church and have kids, as if those dreams could distract from the real conversation. Honestly, I think it confused me more than it confused her.

She gave me a big hug. Told me she loved me.

And that moment—however complicated—meant everything.

Because up until that point, I had braced for rejection. I was prepared for the kind of silence that slices, for the kind of disappointment you can't un-hear. But instead, I got arms around me. I got words of love. It didn't erase the pressure, the religious overtones, or the unspoken expectations still hanging in the air. But it reminded me that even in confusion and discomfort, love could still show up.

And then... we never spoke about it again.

Because that's how it works in Hispanic families. You bury the shame, slap a rosary on it, and pray it away. Then you serve arroz con pollo and pretend like the trauma's been exorcised.

My sister—deeply religious and wildly confident in her theology degree from the Church of "I Heard It Somewhere"—told me I needed to get closer to God. That I should go to church more often. That I should seek guidance from a priest.

Now, let's pause for a second.

This was during a time when the media was erupting with exposés about the Catholic Church's systemic cover-up of sexual abuse cases. The Vatican was in full-blown crisis mode. Priests were being shuffled around like deck chairs on the Titanic. And here I was, being told to bring my tender, queer heart to *Father ProbablyNeedsAnInvestigation* for spiritual direction?

Absolutely not.

I may have been emotionally vulnerable, but I wasn't stupid.

And then there was Antonio.

We never talked about it—not once. Not a single word passed between us about who I was or who I loved. But his silence? Somehow, it felt like acceptance. He didn't change. He didn't avoid me. He didn't walk on eggshells or make backhanded comments. He just kept showing up. He kept driving me places, asking about school, handing me $20 like it was nothing. And that, in its own quiet way, meant more to me than any sermon or speech. It wasn't overt affirmation, but it also wasn't rejection. And at the time, that felt like a win.

Next came the confrontation I'd been avoiding for as long as I could—my brother. I didn't know whether to loathe him for outing me or thank him for finally flinging open the closet door and flipping on the light. It was one of those "choose your own trauma" moments. The scene? His 1995 black Nissan Sentra. The attitude? Corvette. He whipped that car around like it had turbo. It didn't.

It was 2006.

I remember the words like they were etched into my bones:

"You will never succeed if you choose that lifestyle."

Nine words. That's all it took.

At first, they knocked the air out of me. I sat there, stunned, feeling the weight of his judgment settle like concrete in my chest. And for a moment, I believed him. For a moment, I wondered if he was right.

But then something shifted. Those nine words didn't just wound me—they lit a fire. They became my fuel. The voice in the back of my head when I got into college. When I crossed the graduation stage. When I earned my master's. When I was recognized, promoted, celebrated. When I stood in rooms I had once only dreamed of entering—and *owned* them. Every accolade I earned, every milestone I reached, every moment of pride became a quiet rebellion against his sentence:

"You will never succeed…"

Watch me.

Chapter Eight

UCF – University of Coming (Out) Free

Coming out didn't come with a parade. It came with conditions—hugs wrapped in hesitation, love that felt like it came with an asterisk. After all the awkward conversations, the unsolicited Bible verses, and the silence that echoed louder than any scream, I realized something: I couldn't keep becoming in the same place where I'd spent so long hiding.

I needed space. I needed freedom. I needed to build a version of myself that didn't come with footnotes and disclaimers. And for that, I had to go.

By the end of high school, I'd been accepted to my first-choice school: the University of Central Florida in Orlando. I chose UCF like I was drafting an escape plan and a budget spreadsheet at the same time. It was the perfect distance from my family—close enough to keep my in-state tuition *(thank you, Bright Futures)*, but far enough to finally exhale.

The campus looked like it had been lifted straight from a "Modern Collegiate Chic" catalog—sleek glass buildings, clean lines, and not a single Gothic gargoyle in sight. Orlando promised a lively city scene, actual nightlife, and more quirky pop-up adventures than any sleepy strip mall could offer. And, let's be honest, the possibility of spontaneous weekends at theme parks where adults can wear Mickey ears without judgment? Irresistible.

Thanks to an arsenal of scholarships—academic, leadership, community service—I ended up getting refund checks after tuition, books, and housing were covered. A literal paycheck for being excellent. *(Shoutout to Ms. Lucas, who taught me how to finesse both a résumé and a system.)*

Because I'd pulled off the impossible—getting into college and paying for it without needing a single co-signed loan—I negotiated a deal with Julia and Antonio: if they didn't have to pay for tuition, they'd buy me a car.

And they did. The funds came from the trust my mother left me—the one I technically wasn't supposed to touch yet, but they had access to. So I chose a car that balanced my taste with their obsession over safety: a silver 2007 Toyota Camry SE. Sleek. Dependable. Respectable. It was my baby.

The first time I slid behind the wheel and turned the ignition, it wasn't just transportation—it was liberation. I could leave when I wanted, blast Lady Gaga at max volume, or sit in a parking lot with the A/C on and no one asking what was on my mind. It wasn't just a car. It was the first thing that ever felt entirely mine.

I started classes in the summer of 2007 and moved into The Towers at Knights Plaza—sleek, apartment-style residence halls nestled right next to the campus arena. My unit, like most, was a four-bedroom, two-bath setup with a furnished living room, a full kitchen (dishwasher included), and private bedrooms with full-size beds. For a first taste of college life, it felt like luxury.

But the dream was short-lived.

By fall, on-campus housing was maxed out, and I got bumped to a waitlist. So I had to find off-campus housing—fast. That's how I ended up at Pegasus Pointe, in the all-freshman building. It was a chaotic little ecosystem of ramen dinners, late-night laughter echoing down the halls, and wide-eyed kids tasting freedom for the first time.

And I struck gold.

All three of my roommates were straight, friendly, well-mannered— and, bonus—extremely attractive. Lucky me.

But let me be clear: they were eye candy, not a menu. I've never bought into the "flip the straight guy" fantasy. I abhor the idea. I wasn't looking for a project—I wanted a partner.

Fortunately for them, I made girlfriends quickly, which meant they had a steady rotation of cute women to flirt with. *You're welcome, boys.*

What I didn't know when I chose UCF was that I'd unintentionally landed in a queer-friendly haven. Orlando wasn't just theme parks and sunshine—it was a low-key gay mecca. San Francisco may have had the reputation, but Orlando had the heart, the allyship, the community, and the vibe.

On campus, there was a student organization called the Gay, Lesbian, and Bisexual Student Union—GLBSU. It was loud, proud, and exactly what I needed: a space to be curious, connected, and fully myself.

Ms. Lucas's lessons from high school echoed in my head, so I did what she taught me—I joined. I showed up. I made friends. And little by little, I began unlearning the parts of myself I'd kept small for far too long.

Off campus, there was *Pulse Nightclub*. But Pulse wasn't just a nightclub. It was church. It was sanctuary. A place where the music pulsed like a heartbeat, where drag queens were celestial beings, and where you could dance next to strangers and still feel like family. It stood for joy, resistance, identity, and freedom—all under one electrified, neon roof.

To me, it was all of that and so much more: First dates. Blue Long Islands that were way too strong. Drag performances that left me speechless. And nights I don't entirely remember—but will never forget.

Of course, the world knows Pulse now for a very different reason. On June 12, 2016, a gunman entered the club during "Latin Night" and opened fire. Forty-nine people were killed, fifty-three were injured. At the time, it was the deadliest mass shooting in U.S. history and one of the most violent attacks on the LGBTQ+ community this country had ever seen. It shattered something in us. And it shattered something in me.

But before tragedy rewrote its legacy, Pulse was where I was supposed to meet the guy who became my first boyfriend.

Technically, we didn't meet there—we met on MySpace. His name was Miles, and his profile photo made me hit 'Add Friend' faster than I care to admit. He was cute. Cool. Cryptic. We exchanged messages for a few days and made plans to meet up at Pulse one night. It felt casual—but electric. Like, *this could actually become something.*

Except I chickened out.

I spotted him across the room with his friend. He looked even better in person. I panicked, downed one of those dangerously neon Blue Long Islands, and tucked myself into a corner with my own crew—too shy, too nervous, caught in that liminal space between craving connection and not yet knowing how to be *seen.*

That night, when I got home, I saw a message from him. He had sent me his number earlier that evening. After a moment of pacing around my room like I was defusing a bomb, I texted him.

Turns out, he was at a friend's apartment—*just across the street.* So I mustered up the courage, got back in my car, and drove over.

At first, we all hung out outside the apartment—just me, him, and his friend. Eventually, they invited me in. We talked for a bit, until his friend went to bed, leaving the two of us alone.

And then… something clicked.

We talked for hours. The kind of conversation that melts time. No awkward silences. No performative small talk. Just an unfolding. I remember walking out of that apartment thinking, *Damn, he's hot.* But it wasn't just the looks—it was everything else. (Although, let's be real, the looks didn't hurt.)

Miles was 6'2"—just a few inches taller than me—with a lean frame, the kind of body shaped more by purpose than vanity. His jawline was sharp, but softened by gentle Native American features that made his face feel both grounded and ethereal. His lips were full, the kind you see on magazine covers, and his olive-toned skin looked practically airbrushed in real life. And his hair? Long enough to run your hands through—soft, thick, and perfectly tousled, like it belonged in a moody indie film.

Oh—and he was pursuing modeling on the side. Because of course he was.

But he wasn't just beautiful. He was focused. Smart. Artistic. Thoughtful. He was studying to become a doctor while working overnight shifts as a CNA at a hospital. He had ambition, and a quiet confidence that made you want to lean in and listen.

We agreed to hang out again and kept texting in the days that followed. Our conversations grew longer, deeper, more personal.

But there was one tiny hiccup—or maybe a *pink flag:* he lived in Titusville. About 45 minutes away. Not exactly long-distance, but far enough to complicate things once feelings started getting involved. And make no mistake… feelings were definitely getting involved.

The following week, we made plans to go to Pulse. Oblivious me thought we were going with the same friend I'd met the week before, so imagine my surprise when Miles showed up alone at my apartment. I opened the door and immediately asked, *"Where's your friend?"* He just smiled, cool and confident, and said, *"It's just me."* And just like that, the butterflies in my stomach went from dormant to full-blown Cirque du Soleil.

We arrived at Pulse later that night, and to this day, it remains one of my most vivid memories. The music, the lights, the energy—it all buzzed like static under my skin. Partway through the night, a drag queen took the stage and began lip syncing "No One" by Alicia Keys. I don't know what it was—her performance, the electricity in the room, the way the lyrics cut through everything—but something about that moment felt magical.

Miles pulled me close as she "sang" with all the drama and soul of a Broadway diva. His arms wrapped around me, and for the first time, I didn't flinch or glance over my shoulder. I let myself be held. And then it happened. He looked at me—really looked—and kissed me. Just like that, the club, the crowd, the world melted away.

His lips were exactly as I'd imagined: full, soft, like velvet wrapped around a promise. It wasn't rushed or clumsy. It was slow, deliberate—the kind of kiss that makes your knees forget how to function. The kind that settles in your chest and rewires something.

It didn't feel like a first kiss. It felt like a permission slip. To be seen. To be wanted. To be exactly who I was. And in that moment, with Alicia Keys soaring in the background and the bass shaking the floor beneath us, I didn't feel afraid. I didn't feel judged. I felt... free.

Shortly after that first night at Pulse, we started seeing each other regularly. Beach dates, movie nights, late-night drives. He introduced me to sushi. I introduced him to my unfiltered opinions. We traveled—a lot.

Time for a Commercial Break…

Once I settled into the full rhythm of college life, I realized I had too much time and not enough money. So, I decided to get a job.

I spent days scouring the UCF area with no luck—apparently, every other college student had beaten me to it. Desperate and mildly dramatic, I expanded my search radius and landed at American Eagle in The Mall at Millenia, about 20 miles away. I walked in, résumé in hand, and the manager—who just so happened to be gay—hired me on the spot. Did my tight jeans and encyclopedic knowledge of seasonal layering help? Let's just say... God gives his strongest discount codes to his favorite gays.

It wasn't the worst gig. I stayed long enough to abuse the 50% employee discount and stock my closet like I was prepping for Fashion Week: College Edition. But eventually, the sparkle faded. My manager (not the fun gay one) turned out to be an insufferable, power-tripping nightmare.

So I did what any overachieving, underpaid college student with dreams would do: I found something better.

My next job actually aligned with my major at the time— Hospitality Management. I got hired at the Homewood Suites by Hilton near UCF. Best. Decision. Ever. It was walking distance from my apartment. I got to practice Spanish with the housekeeping staff, network with actual professionals, and—here's the kicker—my employee hotel discount felt like legal theft. *Thank you, Hilton Honors gods.*

I ended up working there for four and a half years, eventually becoming Front Office Manager. Nearly my entire college career happened in that building, and honestly, I loved every minute of it.

Until I didn't.

Because once I imagined giving up every weekend, holiday, and major life event in exchange for complimentary cookies at check-in... I realized this wasn't the forever plan.

But that job did give me something priceless—the freedom to travel. And more importantly, the freedom to travel with *him*.

...*Commercial Break Over.*

We took trips to Miami, Key West, Pensacola, Atlanta, New York, and even Helen, Georgia—a tiny Bavarian-inspired village nestled in the Blue Ridge Mountains, full of German food, kitschy shops, and enough lederhosen décor to make you question reality. But nothing—nothing—topped New York.

We went during the winter of 2008 with one mission: to watch the ball drop in Times Square on New Year's Eve. We did all the quintessential New York things—climbed the Empire State Building, toured Rockefeller Center, waved at Lady Liberty, and even made a nostalgic detour to Coney Island, where I had grown up. But the ball drop was the main event.

We arrived around 2 p.m.—yes, in the afternoon—to claim our spot. What no one told us back then (and absolutely should have) was that once you were barricaded into a section near the drop zone, you couldn't leave. If you did, you lost your spot and got sent to the back of the line—which basically meant New Jersey.

So, we did what had to be done: made one last desperate bathroom run, then bundled up and braved the freezing cold. Our bladders were full, our toes numb, and anticipation built with every countdown hour.

And then the moment came. Ten... Nine... Eight... The crowd roared. Confetti burst into the air like a million tiny promises. Three... Two... One...

The ball dropped.

Miles turned to me—his eyes soft and sure—and said, *"I love you,"* for the first time. It wasn't loud. It didn't need to be. It was the kind of "I love you" that hushes the world. That makes your heart skip and settle in the same breath. That plants something in you you didn't even know was missing—until it bloomed.

He kissed me right there, in the middle of Times Square, in a sea of strangers. And for that moment, we weren't just faces in the crowd— we were the main characters in our own little love story.

Shortly after, we made a beeline for the nearest train and headed back to Brooklyn, where my family was gathered. He met them that night. And they loved him.

It was the first time I'd ever introduced a boyfriend to my family—and it wasn't just accepted, it was celebrated. At the time, my family in New York was far more open and affirming than my immediate family in Florida. In Brooklyn, I felt like I had come home. And more importantly, they made him feel like he belonged too.

For the first time in my life, I knew what it meant to be fully seen—and fully embraced. And in that season—of becoming, of falling, of learning to live out loud—I believed I had found the kind of love that would carry me into the next chapter of my life.

What I didn't yet understand was that love, like identity, doesn't always arrive in its final form. But I was beginning to learn that even the temporary can leave permanent marks. And Miles' name would be one I'd carry with me—long after the kiss, long after the countdown, long after the confetti had fallen.

Chapter Nine

The First Goodbye I Never Got Right

At the time, I thought I had found it—the kind of love novels are written about and playlists are built for. The kind that feels like forever when you're standing in Times Square, wrapped in someone's arms, lips still buzzing from that first "I love you," with confetti falling like blessings from the sky. I was young, in love, and—for the first time in my life—I felt chosen.

Everything about Miles felt like possibility. Our story started like a rom-com: late-night texts, inside jokes, beach dates, spontaneous road trips. He had this calm energy, a quiet confidence that made me feel safe, grounded, wanted. We danced under club lights and kissed like we had something to prove—to the world, to ourselves. And in that moment, I believed in us. Completely.

But what I didn't understand back then was that love—the kind that lasts—isn't sustained by grand gestures or perfect moments. It's built in the in-between. It's in the follow-through. The unglamorous parts.

The hard conversations, the miscommunications, the days when the butterflies are gone, when someone forgets to call, when your love language isn't being spoken at all. Love is a choice you make—again and again—even when it's difficult.

No one teaches you how to love someone else while you're still learning how to love yourself. There's no syllabus for your first real relationship. You just dive in—heart first, eyes closed—and hope you don't drown.

I thought he was my soulmate. I truly did. But what I've come to understand is that soulmates don't always stay. Sometimes, they show up to crack something open inside you. To awaken something. To teach you a lesson you didn't know you needed. And when that lesson's over, they leave you standing there—different, raw, a little broken… but also, somehow, more whole.

Our last trip together was to Helen, Georgia. I didn't know it would be our last. I certainly didn't plan on it. I still loved him. And despite the distance that had crept in—despite the miscommunications, the missed calls, the quiet tension—I knew, deep down, he still loved me too.

But I made a mistake. I started listening more to the noise outside of us than the voice inside of me. I confided in friends—some well-meaning, some just messy enough to stir the pot—and they gave me the kind of advice that sounds empowering… until it leaves you empty.

"Leave him."

"You can do better."

"He's not showing up for you."

And maybe they weren't entirely wrong. But love doesn't always respond well to logic. So when Miles started to slip into silence, when he stopped telling me what he needed and left me guessing through the cold space growing between us—I left. Not with anger. Not with malice. Just... exhaustion.

I didn't want to do the emotional labor anymore. I was tired of feeling like I was loving for two. So I walked away—quietly, stubbornly— expecting him to come after me. To fight for us. To prove, once and for all, that I was his person.

He didn't.

The morning we broke up is still burned into my memory. He had to leave for work, and I had already decided I couldn't hold it in any longer. I had to say it. I had to end it. So I did. I told him I was letting him go. And that's when something cracked.

He broke down crying in a way I had never seen before. His face twisted in hurt and disbelief, tears falling faster than words. And all he could manage to say—between breaths and sobs—was: *"Get out!"* Just like that. One sentence. Sharp. Shaking.

I had never seen that side of him before, and it gutted me. In that moment, I realized how much pain he'd been carrying in silence. How much he had held back. And I hated that I was the one who brought it to the surface—not to heal it, but to break it open.

It hurt more than I expected. Not because he yelled. But because I never wanted to be the reason someone I loved looked like that. That moment stayed with me—etched into a part of me that still aches.

Because I don't ever want to make someone feel that kind of pain again. Especially not someone I once called home.

Before I said the words, I had written a letter to myself—an emotional permission slip—trying to convince myself this was the right decision. That I was choosing myself. That walking away meant strength.

But the truth? I was fighting it the whole time. Every sentence was a scream I tried to dress up as self-respect. I didn't want to let him go. I just wanted him to stop making me feel like I wasn't enough.

I wanted him to reach for me. To ask me to stay. To tell me he was hurting, that he needed me, that we could fix it.

But he didn't.

And what I didn't realize then—what still guts me a little now— is that maybe *he* was hurting. Maybe he was going through something. And I wasn't listening. I was too wrapped up in what I wasn't getting, too tangled in my own fear of being unwanted, to notice that maybe he needed me to fight for him the way I wanted him to fight for me.

That's the thing about first love: it doesn't just teach you how to open your heart. It teaches you what it means to care for someone beyond your own needs. It teaches you how easy it is to confuse silence with apathy… when sometimes, it's just pain. And by the time I figured that out—Miles was already gone.

For a while, I was fine. I even felt liberated, like I'd done the hard thing and was free to start over. But freedom can be deceiving. It feels like healing… until the past knocks on your door—or, in my case, your inbox.

He reached out.

At first, it felt casual. Familiar. Safe. We danced around anything real, texting about Lady Gaga's new album, dissecting tracks from Ingrid Michaelson's latest project. Music had always been our language—the place where we understood each other best.

So I took it as a sign—he missed me. He wanted to reconnect. Maybe my plan had worked. Maybe this was our second chance.

But I was wrong. What he wanted was… *intimacy*. Not reconciliation. Not clarity. Not love. Just someone he trusted. Someone he knew would be gentle. Someone he could do *that* with.

I convinced myself it meant more—that it had to mean more. That if I let it happen, it would draw us back together. That maybe this was how broken love got rebuilt: quietly, privately, one night at a time. But when it was over… that was it. That's all it ever was to him—a moment. A comfort. A memory he didn't care to revisit.

One night, parked outside my apartment, he told me what I wasn't ready to hear. He had started seeing someone else. He didn't think he'd be around much anymore. And he could tell—I was catching feelings again.

He said it gently, but it hit like a gut punch. Because he wasn't wrong. And it broke me. Again.

And maybe you're reading this thinking, *Chris, what were you doing? How could you let him back in? Why would you go through that again?* And I get it. I really do. I must've sounded like a masochist.

But this—*this*—was my journey. And I promised myself I'd tell it exactly as it happened. Messy. Human. Honest. Because what's the point of writing your truth if you're only going to polish the pain until it shines like something it never was?

So yes—I let him back in. I held on to the hope that he'd realize what we had was worth fighting for. And when he didn't... I let go. For real this time. Not out of anger. Out of quiet resignation.

We stopped talking. Again. But not forever. Because here's the thing no one tells you about soulmates—sometimes, they're not the person you spend your life with. Sometimes, they're the person who teaches you what love is *supposed* to feel like... right before they show you everything it's not.

We tried to move on. Tried to stay away. But there was always something—some invisible thread pulling us back into each other's orbit.

A birthday message. A song we both posted without knowing. A meme so specific it could only make sense to the two of us. The kind of thing that reminds you that no matter how much time passes... they still know you.

He was the first person I ever let see *all* of me—before I even fully knew who "me" was. And to this day, I don't know if I was in love with *him*... or in love with the version of *myself* I was when I was with him.

The version who didn't flinch when someone reached for my hand. The version who believed in forever. The version who thought love alone could be enough.

And maybe that's why he lingered in the background of my life—not as a shadow, but as a soft echo. A *what-if.* A once-upon-a-time that never quite faded into "The End."

Even now, with so much life between us, something always stirs—a lyric, a memory, a look. We're not lovers. We're not strangers. We exist in this space without a label, only a history.

And even when I found someone else... he was still there. A ghost in the background. Watching. Waiting. Quiet. A presence I couldn't fully silence. A comparison I didn't mean to make.

But that's the thing about ghosts—eventually, you have to stop chasing them... or risk losing the living love that's right in front of you.

I wish I could say that after Miles, I gave myself time to heal. That I sat with the grief, unpacked the pain, and came out the other side stronger, wiser, and ready. But I didn't.

Because when someone leaves a space in your heart, it's human nature to try and fill it. And I filled it quickly—with someone new. Someone kind. Someone consistent. Someone who made me laugh in quiet moments and helped me forget the sound of someone else's silence. He didn't feel like a firework—he felt like a sunrise.

Slow. Steady. Safe.

But even the gentlest light can cast unexpected shadows.

Chapter Ten

A Ring, a Degree, and the Ghost I Brought Home

My relationship with Miles ended in the fall of 2009, leaving a hollow ache in my chest that felt as vast and empty as the spaces between stars. Instead of sitting with that ache and processing the loss, I tried desperately to fill the void—like patching a bullet hole with a bandage.

Just a few months later, I found myself staring at the soft blue-and- pink glow of my laptop screen, carefully crafting an OkCupid profile at two in the morning. My username? StudMuffin25. Captivating, I know. The profile itself was brutally honest—more a blunt autobiography than a dating pitch. It was unapologetically me, a "this is who I am, take it or leave it" kind of introduction.

One section asked, *"I spend a lot of time thinking about…"* and my answer was honest—maybe too honest. I admitted I often thought about my family. We had drifted apart since I left for college, and the distance only grew when I started dating Miles. My family refused to acknowledge that part of my life, so out of pride—or maybe self-preservation—I stopped acknowledging them altogether. Still, buried beneath the silence was a quiet hope that someday things might change. And eventually, they did. Time has a way of stitching broken pieces back together when you least expect it.

Night after night, I scrolled through profiles, reading bios illuminated by the soft, bluish glow of my screen. Every profile felt like a gamble, another hopeful click into possibility, another chance to quiet the loneliness humming just beneath the surface. I didn't know it then, but hidden among those endless matches and late-night browsing sessions, I would find the person I'd spend the next four and a half years of my life with—Lyric.

I messaged him first, mostly because he was one of my top matches—93% compatible, according to OkCupid's seemingly magical algorithms. More impressive than the percentage, though, was his profile. It read like the first chapter of a novel I already knew I wanted to finish.

By then, I had switched my major to English Language Arts Education, so naturally, I was drawn to someone who could weave words with thoughtfulness and skill. But there were two glaring red flags—or maybe just flashing caution lights. First, Lyric lived in Jacksonville, a solid two-hour drive from Orlando. Second—and perhaps even more alarming—he owned a Blackberry instead of an iPhone. Clearly, I was shooting for the stars and hoping gravity was on my side.

We started messaging in mid-March of 2010, tentative at first, but soon our exchanges grew deeper—long paragraphs filled with stories, secrets, and laughter. Each night, our conversations stretched into the early morning hours, until the sun reminded us we should have gone to sleep hours ago. Before long, weekends belonged entirely to us. Lyric would brave the highway from Jacksonville, or I would drive north, savoring the anticipation with every passing mile marker.

When we finally met in person, my heart confirmed what my intuition already knew—I was falling, fast. Lyric was white, my height, with blond hair, striking green eyes, and a quirky sense of humor that matched mine perfectly. He had an infectious laugh—the kind that pulled you into joy even when you didn't quite get the joke—and an easygoing charm that felt like sunlight.

As if that weren't enough, he was musically gifted; he could play the piano effortlessly and sing like he had stepped straight out of a rom-com montage. I was smitten. I was enchanted. I was in love.

For a while, the distance worked beautifully, but eventually, I grew restless. I wanted more than weekend visits, more than borrowed time. I wanted Lyric close. Permanently. So naturally, only a month after we started talking, I asked him to be my boyfriend. Yes, we were officially moving at lesbian speed. *(Don't worry—the U-Haul was practically already parked outside.)*

I asked him through a handwritten letter tucked inside a small, velvet-lined box. Inside that box was my high school ring—silver and engraved, a token from the years when I first learned what happiness felt like. I had worn it faithfully, almost superstitiously, as a reminder of who I had become during those formative years.

But as I placed it inside that box, I realized I no longer needed it. Lyric had become my happiness—my new anchor. At the bottom of the letter, I carefully wrote, *"I found my Prince Charming."* My heart raced with nervous excitement as I sealed it, hoping he'd understand exactly what that gesture meant.

When he received it, Lyric didn't hesitate—not for a second. He accepted immediately, slipping my silver ring onto his finger, a tangible promise between us. In that moment, all the distance, uncertainty, and red flags faded into the background. Just like that, we were official—and I felt like I had finally stepped into the love story I'd always imagined.

At the time, Lyric was deciding between attending the University of Florida in Gainesville or joining me at the University of Central Florida to pursue Political Science and International Affairs. Anxious and impatient, I did what any reasonable, emotionally stable twenty-something would do— I issued an ultimatum: either he came to UCF, or we wouldn't have a future together. *(Who the hell did I think I was back then?)*

But somehow, I got my wish. Lyric chose UCF, and within just a few months, we were signing a lease together, moving boxes into our very first apartment—a cozy one-bedroom unit tucked into a quiet corner of Winter Park, right on the outskirts of campus. *(See? I told you that U-Haul was on its way.)* We furnished the space quickly, turning empty walls and bare rooms into something straight out of an IKEA showroom, complete with framed posters, matching dinnerware, and a modest wine rack stocked with whatever was on BOGO at Publix, convinced it made us look far more grown-up than we actually were.

It felt surreal. It felt like we were winning at adulting. It felt like the beginning of a forever neither of us questioned, because in those early days, nothing mattered beyond the boundaries of our carefully decorated apartment and the comforting rhythm of sharing life with someone new.

For years, I told myself I had forgotten about Miles. I wrapped that chapter of my life in metaphorical bubble wrap, sealed it in a box labeled *"do not reopen,"* and shoved it into the back corner of my heart. I convinced myself I was genuinely happy with my new life, my new love, my new rhythm with Lyric.

And for the most part, I was.

Just not entirely.

Because something was missing.

There were days when everything looked perfect on paper. I had the boyfriend. The apartment. The candlelit dinners and the matching towel sets from Target. But then there were other days—quiet ones— when a memory would slip through the cracks. A song. A smell. A dream I couldn't shake. And suddenly, I was right back where I started.

I went through an endless cycle of blocking and unblocking Miles on social media. It became almost ritualistic. I would convince myself I was over it, that I could handle seeing his posts—photos with friends, gym selfies, vague status updates that felt like they were written for me (even though I knew they weren't). But then the ache would creep in. The shame. The guilt. The haunting question: *Was I the villain in his story?*

And so, I blocked him again. Not because I hated him, but because I hated the way I still missed him. Yet something always pulled me back to him. *(Cue "Gravity" by Sara Bareilles.)*

It was never one big thing—just little ones. A song we used to sing in the car. A wine that tasted like his lips, smooth and a little dangerous. The silence of a Sunday afternoon that felt too heavy without his laughter. He lingered like a ghost—not angry, not bitter, just... unfinished.

Still, I kept going. I poured myself into the life Lyric and I were building together, and we settled into a rhythm that mirrored a married couple in all the domestic, oddly satisfying ways.

We planned our meals every Sunday night—chicken marsala, penne alla vodka, pork chops with a mango glaze *(thank you, Publix Aprons)*. I usually cooked because I loved it, and because Lyric—bless his heart—was white, and seasoning wasn't exactly his forte.

He handled the laundry and cleaning; his schedule was more flexible, and frankly, he folded a fitted sheet better than anyone I'd ever met. Our days became predictable in the best way. Friday nights were sacred—we'd dress up and try a new fine dining spot somewhere in Orlando, sip overpriced martinis, and pretend we understood tannins when we switched to wine. We talked like food critics, raised our eyebrows at the plating, and nodded at flavor pairings like we weren't going to eat cereal at midnight anyway.

Saturdays were for adventure. We'd meet up with friends, shop at The Mall at Millenia or wander IKEA (again), or hit one of the theme parks we had annual passes to—two big kids eating overpriced churros and coming home with sunburns.

Sundays were slower. Softer. Farmer's markets in the morning, where we bought produce we couldn't pronounce simply because it looked "aesthetic." Grocery runs in the afternoon, where we debated almond milk brands and impulse-bought snacks we didn't need (but always justified).

Eventually, we ditched our usual stores and upgraded to Whole Foods—mainly for the wine bar with a tapas menu that made us feel like we had our lives together. Grocery shopping after a bottle of wine was dangerous and delightful. The total at the register? It cost more than our dignity. Then home, where we'd decompress with movies, wine, and the occasional bottomless Sunday Funday brunch that turned into spontaneous karaoke—him on piano, me belting Adele like I had clearly not read the room.

We had built a life. A good one.

But even in all that goodness, even in the laughter and routines and Instagrammable brunches, a part of me still looked over my shoulder. Not out of regret. Not even longing. But because there was a version of myself still trying to catch up. And sometimes, no matter how far forward you move, the past still has a pulse.

In August 2012, I graduated with my Bachelor's in English Language Arts Education and a minor in Business Administration. It took me five years, partly because of that minor—I figured if I was serious about becoming a principal one day, understanding budgets and bureaucracy wouldn't hurt. I also took a semester off after my breakup with Miles. Coincidence? I think not.

I planned my graduation the way most people plan weddings: professional catering, custom décor, a dance floor, and enough seating charts to make your head spin. Thankfully, I used my hotel as the venue.

I sent out 120 invitations—and every single person showed up. For me. It was overwhelming in the best way. I was proud. I had done it. I had crossed a major milestone and built something for myself, one class, one job, one sleepless night at a time.

But pride wasn't the only thing sitting in my chest that day. Because I had another plan. One even bigger than graduation. I had decided I was going to propose to Lyric.

I bought the ring—$1,500 and a small identity crisis later—and convinced myself this was the next chapter. It made sense. We had built a life together. It was comfortable. It was safe. And I thought maybe, just maybe, it was enough.

But for weeks leading up to that moment, I had been hiding something—something not even my closest friends knew. I had let Miles back in. Not just in messages. Not just in memory. In person.

He still lived in Orlando. We were in the same city, quietly orbiting each other, until I opened the door again.

It was a weekday. Lyric was at work. And I told myself I just needed closure. Clarity. Something clean to carry with me as I moved forward. But the truth? I missed him. And the second I saw him, that ache—the one I thought I'd buried—roared back to life.

We didn't talk much. We didn't need to. Some part of me just wanted to feel close to him again, even if it was fleeting. And for a little while, I did. Our bodies said everything our mouths couldn't. We slipped into something familiar—something I had no business revisiting—but I went anyway.

And then… he left.

And I threw up.

I literally ran to the bathroom and got sick—body shaking, heart pounding, drowning in shame.

What had I done!?

I was about to propose to someone else. Someone who loved me. Someone who showed up. And I betrayed him—without warning, without reason, without excuse.

I blocked Miles again. Shut the door. Buried the evidence. But the guilt? That didn't go anywhere. It sat with me. It gnawed at me. It tainted everything good I tried to hold onto. Because deep down, I knew I had made a choice I couldn't undo. And the worst part? I still wasn't sure who I had betrayed more—Lyric… or myself.

I wish I could say that moment—the nausea, the guilt, the shame—was enough to make me confront the truth. To really sit with it. But grief is a master of disguise. It doesn't always show up in tears and tissues. Sometimes it wears the mask of impulse, distraction, denial. Sometimes it looks like a door you should've kept closed—but didn't.

In an earlier chapter, I talked about loss—how it doesn't just disappear when you ignore it. How pain, when left unprocessed, doesn't dissolve. It waits. Quietly. Patiently. It finds the cracks in your foundation and seeps in. And when it does? It doesn't knock. It kicks the door in.

That was the moment for me.

I had never dealt with the grief of losing Miles. Not really. I had shoved it into the back of my mind, buried it under routines, wine bar brunches, IKEA furniture, and a life that looked good from the outside. But grief doesn't care how polished your new life looks. If it's unresolved, it will find you—and it will unravel you from the inside out.

I thought I had moved on. I thought loving someone new would heal what had broken before. But all I had done was press pause on the pain.

And pain, unspoken and unmet, doesn't just fade.

It ferments. It festers. It follows you.

Until you finally look it in the eye and ask,

What do you want from me?

Pain is patient like that. It waits for the quiet moments—when the music stops, when the guests leave, when the lights go out. That's when it creeps in. Not as a scream, but as a whisper: *You haven't dealt with this.*

And it was right.

I had never truly grieved Miles. Not the end of our relationship, not the version of myself I lost with him, not the dreams we built that never made it past a "what if." I buried those feelings beneath a life that felt more like a performance than a partnership. A good one, yes. A stable one. But sometimes, we confuse peace with the absence of pain. And those aren't the same thing.

The truth is, I had only loved Lyric the way I knew how to at the time—partially. Carefully. Through the lens of someone still haunted by unfinished business. I had poured myself into a new story while leaving whole chapters unread behind me. And that's not love. That's survival.

I thought I was healing. But I was just distracting.

I thought I was moving on. But I was circling back.

I thought I was building a future. But I was still living in the echoes of my past.

It wasn't fair to Lyric. And it wasn't fair to me.

But that's what unprocessed grief does. It convinces you that if you just build something new fast enough, you'll never have to mourn what was lost. You can run from sadness. You can out-organize the ache. You can schedule joy like an appointment and hope it sticks.

But grief? It doesn't play by your schedule. It comes when it's ready. And if you won't let it through the front door, it will sneak in through the cracks.

And in that moment, sitting in a bathroom, sick with guilt, hours after Miles had walked out my door and I had committed to spending forever with someone else—I realized: I hadn't moved on. I had just moved forward… without ever looking back.

Dear Lyric,

I owe you more than an explanation. I owe you an apology. You didn't know the full story. You didn't know that part of my heart was still standing in the wreckage of something unfinished. You didn't know how much I wanted to believe that loving you would be enough to silence everything I hadn't healed.

But I did.

And I still stayed.

And that wasn't fair.

You gave me consistency when my world had only ever taught me chaos. You gave me softness when I was still learning how to receive care without suspicion. You gave me laughter, warmth, partnership, and a version of stability I'd never known before.

And I brought ghosts into our home. Not maliciously. Not to hurt you. But because I hadn't learned yet how to leave the past where it belonged. I was still carrying pieces of another story in my pockets while writing one with you.

I wish I had been braver. I wish I had been clearer. I wish I had told you how broken I still was, instead of pretending I had it all together. You deserved someone whole. And I was still putting my pieces back together, one apology at a time.

If I could go back, I wouldn't rewrite our story—because it mattered. You mattered. But I would have entered it with more honesty. And a heart that was ready to love you the way you deserved to be loved.

I hope you're well. I hope you're happy. I hope you've found the kind of peace I was still searching for back then.

Apologetically,

—Chris

Life, in all its messy, unpredictable brilliance, doesn't wait for you to finish healing before handing you your next milestone. Because despite everything swirling beneath the surface, the day I had been working toward for five long, complicated years had finally arrived. My graduation.

The day of my graduation party felt like a dream I had designed down to the last detail. The food was impeccable, the open bar overflowing, and the music? Curated like a wedding playlist with a little something for everyone. I had created a video tribute honoring my parents—those I had lost too soon—and thanking the family who had held me through the storm and carried me to this moment. There wasn't a dry eye in the room.

In true theatrical fashion, I surprised Julia and Antonio by presenting them with honorary doctorate degrees from the University of Central Florida—printed, framed, and sealed with the kind of pomp and circumstance only a gay college graduate could pull off. I wanted them to feel seen. Celebrated. Because regardless of our complicated past, they had helped me get here.

And then, I dropped one more announcement: I had landed a job. A real job. I was officially an English teacher, starting that Monday. The room erupted in applause. But even with all the love, all the cheers, all the pride pulsing through the room, I hadn't reached the climax just yet.

Because then... came *the* moment. I took the microphone, thanked everyone, and turned to Lyric—the man who, in so many ways, had helped me rebuild. With my heart thudding in my chest and my future staring back at me, I got down on one knee. There, in front of 120 people and under the glow of everything I thought I wanted, I asked him to marry me. He said yes.

The applause felt like thunder. My friends screamed. People cried. Someone probably dropped a drink. And just like that, we danced into the night—two young men caught in a moment that looked and felt like a fairy tale. But fairy tales have chapters we don't always read aloud.

Because what the guests didn't know—what even he didn't know—was that my proposal had been wrapped in guilt, tied with a ribbon of regret. I was trying to write a happy ending with a pen still leaking ink from a story I hadn't closed. The truth has a way of slipping through the cracks, though. No matter how well you patch it up, eventually, it finds the light. And it did.

Months later, Lyric found out. He didn't scream. He didn't throw things. Oh wait—yes, he did. My phone. Into the wall. Left a hole the size of my poor decision-making. And he slapped me across the face. Not metaphorically. Not emotionally. A full, open-palmed slap that knocked the last shred of denial out of me.

The silence that followed? Still deafening. The hurt in his eyes was louder than any accusation—the kind of pain that doesn't need words to make its point. Because in that moment, I wasn't his partner. I was a stranger in the room wearing his heartbreak.

There's a particular kind of devastation that comes when you realize you've become the person you swore you'd never be. When you look at someone you love and know, you did this. And no apology, no explanation, no version of "I didn't mean to" can unring that bell.

He moved out about a year later.

But that year nearly broke me. I was trying to stitch together the pieces of myself I had torn apart, learning how to live with guilt while still trying to be present, to be loving, to be enough. Some days, I showed up with flowers and apologies; other days, I barely recognized the face staring back at me in the mirror. I was forgiving myself in pieces, all while hoping he wouldn't notice the cracks. And still… it wasn't enough.

But deep down, I knew why. Love can't survive when one person is drowning and the other's still bleeding. And just like that, the life we had built together—the routines, the inside jokes, the decorative wine bottles we swore we'd repurpose—was dismantled, one drawer at a time.

We never made it to the wedding. We didn't even make it to the planning phase. And I wish I could tell you I healed immediately. That I learned the lesson and never made another mistake. That this was my rock bottom and I soared after. But grief is stubborn. Growth is slow. And regret? Regret sticks around.

Sometimes the hardest part of becoming isn't just learning from the pain—it's realizing you caused it. And then figuring out how to live with that truth. Every. Single. Day.

When I wrote the preface to this book, I made a promise: that I would tell the truth. Even the uncomfortable parts. Especially the uncomfortable parts.

I said I would show you the curated version of my life—the accolades, the polished smiles—but also the version that hid behind it. The one I buried. The one I tried to rewrite without ever dealing with the chapters I didn't want anyone to read.

This is one of those chapters. I didn't always get it right. I didn't always know how to hold love gently. I made selfish choices. I hurt people. And sometimes, I hurt the very people who loved me the most.

But I'm telling you anyway. Not for pity. Not for praise. But because honesty is the only thing that has ever truly set me free. Because maybe you've made a mess too. Maybe you've said the wrong thing. Stayed too long. Left too soon. Hurt someone you thought you'd never lose. Maybe, like me, you're still learning how to be the version of yourself you want to be.

This—every word of this—is part of that becoming. It's not easy to write about your own failures. It's even harder to admit them. But I believe in the power of speaking truth—not just for healing, but for connection, for redemption, for accountability, for growth.

So if you're still here, still reading, still holding space for me and the flaws I carry—I'm grateful. Because the story doesn't end here. Life, as it tends to do, gave me one more lesson in grief before I had the chance to catch my breath.

In September of 2013, Antonio passed away from esophageal cancer.

It began quietly. He had already outlived the prognosis the doctors had given him, and in typical Antonio fashion, he did so with the kind of quiet strength that made you believe he might beat the odds again. Hospice cared for him at home, just the way he wanted. No sterile hospital room. No machines. Just his recliner, the house he loved, and the people he trusted to carry him through whatever came next.

I spent a week with him in Coconut Creek before he passed. We didn't have some grand, dramatic conversation. But we had something better—something real. Antonio spoke to me the way he always had: through presence, through a nod, through the calm in his voice that said more than words ever could. He didn't have to say *"I love you"* or *"I accept you."* I felt it in the way he looked at me, in the way he told me he was proud of the man I was becoming. That was enough.

After that week, I had to return to work. I told myself he still had time. That I still had time. He'd made it this far—surely, he could hold on a little longer.

That night, Lyric and I decided to go out to dinner (we were still living together at the time). We had barely seen each other all week and needed a brief reprieve from everything. We chose to splurge a little, to pause and try—just try—to feel normal again. Somewhere between appetizers and dessert, I got the call: *"It's time. He's not going to make it."*

I froze.

I sat there in the middle of a crowded restaurant, heart thudding, thoughts racing. And then... I didn't move. I didn't drive back. I didn't rush to be there.

Instead, I stayed.

It's a decision I've replayed in my mind more times than I can count. At the time, it felt like the only choice I had. I had already lived the trauma of losing my mother. Then my father. I knew what it felt like to hold a hand as the pulse faded, to listen for breaths that never came, to pretend to be strong when your world was splitting in half. And I wasn't ready to relive that pain. Not again. Not so soon.

I didn't want my final memory of Antonio to be a deathbed. I wanted it to be that week—the quiet strength, the subtle nods, the unspoken love between us that didn't need fanfare to be real.

By the next morning, I got the call.

He was gone.

I know some of my family didn't understand why I wasn't there in those final moments. Maybe some still don't. But this memoir? It's part of my answer. It's not an excuse—it's an explanation.

I didn't stay away because I didn't care. I stayed away because I cared so deeply, I couldn't bear to watch one more person I loved slip away while I sat helpless. I had to protect what was left of me. Because even warriors have breaking points.

And maybe—just maybe—choosing to remember him as he lived, rather than as he left, was my way of honoring him too.

Antonio's influence didn't vanish with his final breath. It lives on in the quiet ways I move through the world—the way I straighten my posture when I speak, the way I love people deeply without always needing to say the words, because they already know. He taught me that presence isn't always loud. That love, real love, is often steady, unspoken, and unwavering.

Every time I show up for someone who needs to be believed in... every time I offer stability to someone who's never had it... every time I move through this world with both softness and strength... That's him. That's his legacy. Still standing. Still guiding me.

And after that week—after the grief, the guilt, and the goodbye I couldn't bear to witness—what I needed most was air. Not escape, but expansion. A reminder that life doesn't end with loss—it unfolds beyond it. So I leaned into joy. Into motion. Into moments that didn't carry the weight of survival but the spark of something new.

Because sometimes, the heart needs permission to feel light again. And what came next was exactly that—light. Loud. Liberating. Not a forgetting... but a remembering of what it feels like to be alive.

Chapter Eleven

Cruises, Convertibles, and Career Moves

Life can pivot so quickly—from heartbreak to hope, from unraveling to rebuilding. After everything with Lyric, I didn't know what came next. But life doesn't wait for you to feel ready. It moves forward. And so did I.

I started my first job as an English teacher at Lyman High School in Seminole County—a full-circle moment that felt more like fate than coincidence. Just a few months earlier, I had completed my final internship there. To my surprise—and deep gratitude—they offered me a position.

The first person to take a chance on me was Ms. Regina, the assistant principal who hired me. Stern but fair, she carried the kind of presence that made you sit up straighter. Yet beneath her no-nonsense exterior was someone who truly cared. She saw potential in me before I even saw it in myself, and that single "yes" changed the course of my entire career.

Even better, the Reading Department Chair was my former professor from UCF—one of my greatest mentors, Mrs. Stephanie. She nurtured the teacher in me long before I felt ready to claim the title.

I showed up to that classroom nervous but determined, armed with every lesson Ms. Lucas ever taught me—about owning the room, speaking up, and knowing my worth. I wasn't just walking into a school. I was stepping into the version of myself I had worked so hard to become.

At first, I taught English. And I like to think I was good at it. But a few months into the school year, one of the reading teachers resigned—burned out from working with students who had been told, again and again, that they weren't good enough. These were kids stuck in remedial classes simply because they couldn't pass a single standardized test. Kids who were frustrated, angry, disengaged.

And Mrs. Stephanie asked me to take over. It was a big ask for a first-year teacher, but in a school that truly valued student success, the strongest teachers were placed where they were needed most. So, I said yes. And something clicked.

Helping the kids no one else believed in became my calling. I found my rhythm—not just in lesson plans and literacy strategies, but in those quiet moments when a student who used to stare at their desk finally raised their hand. In the breakthroughs. In the trust. It became personal.

Because I had seen what happens when the system fails kids. My brother, Junior, never finished high school. He dropped out—slipped through the cracks, labeled and left behind. And maybe, just maybe, if someone had reached him the way I was trying to reach these kids, things might have been different. So I taught like it mattered. Because it did.

To me, teaching was never just about grammar, essays, or literary analysis. It was about seeing the whole child. It was about walking into a room and saying, *"You are not invisible here."* It was about redemption—about giving what I had once needed.

And somewhere in those rows of desks, surrounded by students the world had written off, I found myself again. Not as someone desperate to prove their worth in love, but as someone who already had it. Teaching gave me purpose when I thought I had lost it. It became my anchor. It became my beginning.

I taught like my heart and life depended on it—because, in many ways, they did. Every lesson plan, every group project, every one-on-one conference was more than curriculum. It was connection. It was my way of reaching students who didn't believe in themselves yet—of showing them that someone saw them, believed in them, and would fight for their success even when they weren't ready to fight for it themselves.

I've always called my students "my kids." Not because I didn't know where professional boundaries were, but because that's what they became—*my kids.* My heartbeat in a classroom. My reason to show up even on the days I felt I had nothing left to give. For many of them, school was the only place they felt safe, the only place they were fed, the only place someone knew their name and said it with kindness. So yes, they were mine. Not in the way parents *own* children, but in the way people take responsibility for what they love.

And then came a full-circle moment that still glows in my memory like warm light in a quiet room.

In my second year at Lyman, I was asked to be the senior class sponsor. It was a massive responsibility—fundraisers, field trips, endless meetings—but I jumped in with both feet. We baked cakes, sold candy grams, organized car washes in the sweltering Florida heat, and begged local businesses for donations. Every dollar felt like a small victory, a step closer to something big.

And then it happened.

We raised enough money to plan their senior prom—not because the school couldn't afford one, but because we wanted to keep costs low while giving them a night they'd never forget. A night that felt like luxury. Like magic. Like the celebration they deserved.

Every dollar we raised was a promise: *You won't have to sit this one out. Not because of money. Not on my watch.*

We booked a stunning venue, chose the perfect theme, and obsessed over every detail—from the color of the napkins to the last song on the playlist.

On prom night, I stood at the edge of the dance floor, watching them laugh, twirl, and sing like the world hadn't bruised them yet. They were radiant. Joyful. Free. And in that moment, I wasn't just their teacher. I was someone who had helped create a memory they'd carry for the rest of their lives.

It felt like redemption. It felt like purpose. And it reminded me, again, why I do what I do. Because for every child who walks into my classroom, I want them to know: *You are seen. You are capable. You are worth the effort.* Every single one of you.

After Lyric moved out, I felt an emptiness I hadn't known in years—but for the first time in almost seven, I didn't rush to fill it. I wasn't in a relationship, and, surprisingly, I didn't crave one. I wanted to sit in the silence. I wanted to figure out who I was without the echo of someone else's voice in the room.

Oscar Wilde once said, *"I think it's very healthy to spend time alone. You need to know how to be alone and not be defined by another person."* I decided I was going to live those words—not just quote them on Instagram. I would embody solitude, not just endure it.

So I started making weekend pilgrimages back to South Florida. Every other Friday, I packed a bag and headed down the turnpike—reconnecting with old friends, slowly rebuilding ties with my family, and learning to be alone without feeling lonely. And one weekend, standing barefoot on the sand with salt air in my lungs and the sun warm on my skin, I felt it—clarity. That unshakable inner knowing that it was time. Time to move back. Time to come home. Not just physically, but emotionally. The universe wasn't screaming at me; it was whispering: *"You're ready."*

That summer, I leaned fully into my newly single life. I booked my first cruise—a quick getaway out of Fort Lauderdale to Key West and Cozumel—with my sister, Madeline. And let me tell you, it was more than just a vacation. It was healing.

Madeline and I hadn't always been close, but something about this trip cracked us open in ways we didn't expect. She was still coming to terms with my sexuality—still asking questions, still figuring things out—but what mattered most was that she was trying. Her effort was deliberate, rooted in love, and fueled, in part, by the respect she had for her boss, a school principal who also happened to be gay. She admired him deeply, and for the first time, I think she could see a version of me that wasn't just *different*, but possible.

The cruise itself was exactly what it needed to be. Not too short. Not too long. Just enough. Long enough for us to reconnect—not just as siblings bound by blood and family obligations, but as friends. We danced until the last song (her favorite), explored every port like locals, ate until we couldn't button our pants, and stayed up way too late ordering room service and having deep, unfiltered conversations. About life. About love. About faith. About family.

Madeline… God, where do I even start?

She is one of the kindest souls I've ever known—the kind of kindness that feels radical in today's world. She doesn't just love her people; she shows up for them. Always. She's a phenomenal speech therapist who somehow manages to love children even more than I do—a high bar, if you know me. She's a mother, a sister, a wife—and she does it all without losing that glimmer in her eye or the warmth in her smile.

Madeline's energy is infectious. She lights up a room before she even opens her mouth. And don't let her fool you—she doesn't drink, not a drop, but she dances like she invented joy. Her spirit is effervescent. She's the kind of person who makes you believe—no, *know*—that you're loved, just by how fully she listens.

She was the one who picked my mother and me up from the hospital the day I was born—our very first ride home, wrapped in hope and possibility. And years later, when life knocked me down, she was still there, picking me up off the floor—sometimes literally, always emotionally. That's who she is. The kind of person you want at both your beginning and your breaking point. And I'm endlessly grateful she's been there for both.

That trip with her didn't just restore our bond—it restored my faith. My faith that maybe, just maybe, I could exist in a world where my family didn't just tolerate who I was, but embraced it. All of it. All of me.

That summer, I traveled a lot. I went to Tampa for my friend Amanda's bachelorette party—Amanda, one of my closest friends from the teaching program at UCF. We met while navigating lesson plans, pedagogy jargon, and the shared trauma of 8:00 a.m. classes, and we'd been inseparable ever since. I've always been "one of the girls," so it felt only fitting to celebrate her the best way I knew how: with a wild, unforgettable weekend.

After that, I took the bride-to-be on a more private, exclusive bachelorette escape to Miami Beach. Then I jetted off to New York, where I reconnected with my dad's side of the family and spent time with my godmother, Joie—one of my mom's closest friends and, in so many ways, her mirror.

Joie is a short, feisty New Yorican badass with enough energy to power a city grid. A civil engineer by trade and a force of nature by design, she is the definition of self-made. Sharp. Direct. Utterly unbothered by anyone's opinions. She knows exactly what she wants and never wastes time pretending otherwise. She's a boss. A fiercely devoted mother and wife. And she has more class than a Bergdorf window in December—polished, iconic, and impossible to ignore.

That weekend with Joie felt like stepping into a warm, familiar embrace—equal parts love, sass, and sparkle. We lounged on the beach like it was our full-time job. We dined at Manhattan's best restaurants, ordering appetizers as if we had Black AmEx cards and zero regrets.

We did the full New York City tourist experience—shopping, snapping photos in front of landmarks I used to pass without a second glance, laughing like kids seeing Manhattan for the first time. And when the sun dipped below the skyline, we turned the city into our dance floor— laughing, twirling, partying like it was midnight on Y2K.

It was the kind of weekend that reminded me joy doesn't have to be loud to be liberating—it just has to be real. Joie gave me that joy. That freedom. That feeling of being tethered to something beautiful and bold, even in my mother's absence.

Spending time with her felt like having a piece of my mom still walking this earth—commanding attention, radiating strength, loving fiercely. It still feels that way. Every time we're together, I feel that same warmth, that same magic—like my mother's spirit is pulling up a seat at the table, laughing with us, reminding me that love like hers never truly leaves.

That summer also brought a first: I was asked to be a bridesman in a wedding. I said yes faster than the actual bride probably did. And to top it off, I flew to California for the first time to visit an old friend.

Then came *San Diego*.

Oh, San Diego. I left my heart there, cradled in the ocean breeze and kissed by the California sun.

As a kid, I used to pass a showroom on 4th Avenue in Brooklyn that displayed a white convertible Ford Mustang. Sleek. Sexy. Impractical. Everything I dreamed of being. To me, it was success in car form.

Fast forward to summer 2014: I land in San Diego, walk to the rental car counter, and what do they hand me? A white convertible Ford Mustang. I could've cried. It felt like the universe handed me the keys and whispered, *"You're on the right path. Now go live your best life."*

San Diego felt like South Florida's cooler, less humid cousin. The food? *Chef's kiss.* The nightlife? Poppin'. The gay scene? Thriving. Everyone was hot—but humble. I was in heaven.

I explored like I wanted to absorb the city into my bloodstream, and the timing couldn't have been better—it just so happened to be Pride weekend. I cruised up and down the coast, wind in my hair, music blaring, living my best rom-com montage.

I even made it to Coronado Island, a little slice of heaven across the bay. I spent an entire day eating, drinking, exploring—living the dream of a foodie on a mission. And at the San Diego Zoo, standing alone among the animals and the magic, I cried. Because for a moment, I could feel my mom beside me. Watching. Smiling.

Later that summer, I flew to Chicago for my 25th birthday with my college girlfriends, Esmy and Elizabeth. We reminisced, laughed until we wheezed, ate like it was our last meal, drank even more wine, and partied like we'd never left undergrad.

I also flew to North Carolina to visit Amanda at her new home, now an army wife. Coincidentally, my high school best friend, Cassie, was nearby visiting her grandparents. Naturally, we had a reunion.

We went canoeing—or rather, Cassie's cousin dragged us down the river while I clung on for dear life. Let's be honest: I'm allergic to manual labor. We went shooting, rode ATVs through the woods, built a bonfire, and lit fireworks under the stars. It was my full-on *country boy summer* moment—and I was here for it.

Before all the traveling, I had officially resigned from my position at Lyman High School. I wasn't sure what was next, and for once, I was okay with that. I just wanted to live. To breathe. To be.

But of course, teaching always finds its way back to me. Throughout the summer, I applied to a dozen schools across Broward County. But the one I really wanted? Monarch High School. My alma mater.

So, I did what I do best—I showed up. Suited up. Walked into the front office with a résumé in hand and confidence radiating like heat off the pavement.

Most of the staff was still there from my student days. They hugged me, caught up, and made sure I met with the principal, even without an appointment. I handed him my résumé, made my case, and when he said there were no positions available, I didn't flinch.

I smiled and said, *"You will—and when you do, I want to be your first call."* I had no idea if that would work. But something in me knew: this was my place. This was my time.

Weeks later, while walking the streets of Coronado Island, I got the call. He asked if I'd taken a job yet. I hadn't. And just like that, he offered me a position teaching English. I nearly dropped my phone right there in the middle of paradise. I accepted without hesitation.

I was going back—not as a student, but as a teacher. A colleague. A mentor. I would be working alongside the very people who had shaped me, including Ms. Lucas, my former guidance counselor and forever champion.

Some people might find it strange to return to the place that watched them grow. But to me? It felt like coming home. That summer wasn't just a season—it was a reckoning. A beautiful, chaotic, healing, affirming reckoning.

I had traveled across time zones and through emotions, rebuilt bridges with my family, and reconnected with people who reminded me who I was before I lost myself in someone else's version of love. I took deep breaths, belly-laughed with friends, cried in hotel bathrooms, danced like nobody was watching (even when they were), and slowly, gently began to feel like myself again.

And then, life handed me a new beginning—back in the city I once ran from, at the very school that shaped me, working side by side with mentors who had once been the adults I needed most. I was no longer chasing healing. I was creating it—in the classroom, in my community, in the mirror.

But healing, I would come to learn, isn't always a straight line. Sometimes, just when you think you've made it to the other side, something stirs beneath the surface—a flicker, a trigger, a whisper of the past—and you realize there are still pieces of the story that haven't been unpacked.

So there I was—a new job, a new car, a new home, and the kind of confidence that comes from surviving the fire. From the outside, I was thriving. But beneath it all, something was brewing. And as I would soon learn, you can only outrun unhealed trauma for so long—until it catches you, fast and furious, and demands to be felt.

Because even in the brightest light, shadows follow. And mine were getting louder. You can't build a new life on top of old wounds—not without something cracking.

I thought I had turned the page, but the next chapter would nearly write me out of my own story.

Chapter Twelve

When the Cracks Start to Show

I gave eight years of my life to Monarch High School—eight years of hauling home stacks of essays, leading Socratic Seminars that sometimes turned into therapy sessions, and pouring everything I had into the minds and hearts of kids who reminded me a little too much of myself.

Monarch wasn't just a job. It was home. A second chapter in my career that gave me a fresh start after heartbreak, after mistakes, after everything I had left behind in Central Florida. It was the school I once walked through as a student, wide-eyed and full of dreams—and now I had returned as a teacher. At first, it felt like I had found my forever.

I taught English, yes—but somewhere along the line, I also became the Speech & Debate coach. I stumbled into it, the way most teachers stumble into "just one more thing" that ends up changing everything. And I fell in love with it—the structure, the strategy, the sound of a student finding their voice for the first time. Debate became a lifeline for many of my kids, and, eventually, it became one for me too.

But while I was helping students find their purpose, I was quietly losing mine.

I applied to a master's program, determined to take the next step— assistant principal, maybe principal one day. But when I didn't get the GRE score I needed, it felt like more than a setback. It felt like a barricade. A message from the universe that no matter how hard I worked, how much I gave—I still wasn't enough.

That's when I started to spiral.

I can't pinpoint the exact day the cracks began to show. It doesn't work like that. It's not one single moment; it's the slow accumulation of them. The missed calls. The unopened emails. The lesson plans half-written or not at all. The wine bottle uncorked "just to unwind" that turned into two. Then three. Then a routine.

I drank to quiet the shame. I spent money to fill the silence. I swiped my card until the overdraft alerts became white noise.

My dating life? A mess. I ran toward red flags like I was chasing a parade, diving into relationships with unavailable men as if one of them might somehow fix what was broken. Spoiler: none of them could.

I started calling out of work more often, crippled by alcohol-induced anxiety that left me paralyzed. I couldn't move. Couldn't breathe. Couldn't teach. I was failing—at my job, at my relationships, at holding myself together. And people started to notice.

One person in particular: Ms. Karleen.

Karleen was my assistant principal, but more than that, she became a friend. She's Jamaican, and if you've ever met a Jamaican woman with a heart of gold and no filter, you'll understand the force that is Karleen. She didn't have a single hair on her tongue. Brutally honest.

Fiercely loyal. If she loved you, she'd fight for you. But if you were messing up? Oh, she'd let you know—with precision and fire.

One morning, after yet another unexplained absence, Karleen called me into her office. And she let me have it. Unceremonious. Unfiltered. Unapologetic.

I don't remember her exact words—just the tone. The disappointment. The sting of someone who cared too much to sugarcoat it. But the truth? I wasn't really there.

I was sitting in front of her, nodding like I was listening, but my mind was miles away. Distant. Underwater. Everything sounded muffled, like the world was moving around me while I stayed frozen in place.

And then she paused.

"Chris… what's wrong?"

I don't know what it is about that question—the one that slips past your armor, the one asked not with judgment, but with love. Something cracked.

"I don't know," I whispered.

And then I broke. The sobbing came fast, violent, guttural—the kind that grabs you by the throat and doesn't let go. Years of grief, shame, and exhaustion finally clawed their way out all at once.

Karleen's face softened instantly. She crossed the room and wrapped me in a hug—tight, maternal, safe. *"We're gonna get you help,"* she said. And she did.

Right then and there, she picked up the phone and called the District's Employee Assistance Program. Within minutes, she had me a same-day appointment with a therapist. She gave me the rest of the afternoon off, told me to breathe, get some food, and talk to someone.

I didn't want to go. Not because I didn't need it, but because I was ashamed. The last time I'd seen a therapist, I was a child, sent to unpack grief too big for my small body after my mom died. It hadn't helped. So I didn't trust it.

But I went anyway. And that appointment changed everything.

The therapist asked a few simple questions... and then I talked. And talked. For two straight hours. It all poured out—the grief I'd never unpacked, the pain of losing my parents, the trauma of growing up too fast, the confusion of coming out, the heartbreak with Miles, the infidelity with Lyric. The guilt. The fear. The longing. All of it.

I left that office exhausted... but lighter. Like I had been holding my breath for years and finally, finally exhaled.

That day didn't fix everything. But it started something. Because healing doesn't happen in a single moment. It happens in the choice to keep showing up—for yourself, for the life you still want, for the people who haven't given up on you.

I had come undone. But now, I was learning how to rebuild. Brick by brick. Breath by breath. Thanks to Karleen, I didn't have to do it alone.

I kept going to therapy—not as often, not as urgently—but enough to keep the mirror clean. Enough to stay grounded when life tried to knock me off balance. These days, I go for maintenance, for check-ins, for those inevitable curveballs life throws just when you think you've found your rhythm.

Therapy stopped being a last resort and became a lifeline. A gift I give myself. A reminder that I am still worthy of healing.

So if you're reading this and wondering whether therapy is for you, let me be clear: it is. Even if you think you're "fine." Even if you were raised to believe you should just "push through." Even if someone once told you that talking about your feelings makes you weak, it doesn't. It makes you wise.

Therapy isn't just for crisis. It's for clarity. It's not about fixing what's broken—it's about tending to what's sacred. It's where you unlearn the lies you were taught about your worth and begin rewriting the truths you deserve to believe.

Maybe it starts with one appointment. One conversation. One breath you didn't even realize you were holding. Maybe you cry. Maybe you don't. Maybe all you do is sit there, fidgeting with your sleeve, and say, *"I don't even know why I'm here."* And that's okay.

You showed up. And that alone? That's brave as hell. We don't heal by accident. We heal on purpose. So whether it's grief, identity, heartbreak, trauma, or just the heavy, messy middle of being human, therapy is not a weakness. It's a weapon. And baby, you deserve to be armed with every tool that brings you peace.

Give yourself that gift. You are worthy of the work.

After therapy—after doing *the work*—things at my job began to shift. Slowly. Steadily. And then, as if the universe wasn't done proving how connected everything is, Karleen threw me another lifeline. Only this time, it didn't look like an intervention. It looked like a new beginning.

A teacher was leaving to pursue her master's degree in Counseling. She taught Spanish and a growing elective program called Latinos In Action (LIA)—a course designed to "empower our amazing youth to lead and strengthen their communities through college and career readiness."

It was bold. Intentional. Transformative. And now… it needed someone to lead it. Karleen chose me.

My Latinos In Action class became sacred ground—the heartbeat of my day. These students, mostly first- and second-generation Latino youth, walked into that classroom with dreams stitched into their backpacks and burdens far too heavy for their age.

But through LIA, they found more than leadership skills. They found themselves.

They mentored elementary students, hosted school-wide cultural events, led community service projects, and showed up in spaces where their voices had once been silenced.

They didn't just step into leadership—they ran toward it. With heart. With pride. With purpose. And in watching them, I began to reclaim my own.

Because every time I encouraged them to speak their truth, I was learning to speak mine. Every time I told them they were worthy of success, I was learning to believe it for myself.

They gave me more than gratitude or good memories—they gave me hope. They reminded me that even when the world tells you you're too broken to lead, you still get to show up. You still get to rise.

And it was their courage that inspired me to try again. Teaching Latinos In Action didn't just restore my passion—it redefined it. This wasn't your typical elective; this was a movement, a mission, a chance to shape the next generation of Latino leaders.

My students weren't just enrolled—they were invested. They carried not just books and backpacks, but legacy, struggle, hope, and grit. Every day, they walked in determined to prove that their voices mattered.

But LIA also brought me something profoundly unexpected. Through a connection with one of my students, I had the rare and humbling opportunity to meet—no, dine—with Supreme Court Justice Sonia Sotomayor.

Yes, *the* Sonia Sotomayor—the first Puerto Rican woman to sit on the highest court in the land. And I didn't just meet her once. I had dinner with her at restaurants. I had Thanksgiving with her. Me.

She was everything I imagined and more—intellectual in the most effortless way, every word like a masterclass. But beneath that sharp, brilliant mind was a warmth that wrapped around you like a hug.

She didn't speak at you—she listened, leaned in, asked questions. She wanted to know about my life, my career, the way I spoke about my students. She told me teaching wasn't just a job, but a service to the soul of this country.

Here I was, a gay Hispanic educator from South Florida, sitting across the table from a Supreme Court Justice—the Justice Sonia Sotomayor—and she was thanking me. I was floored. Humbled. Affirmed in a way that cracked something open in me.

That moment... that dinner... reminded me of who I was. What I was capable of. And why I started teaching in the first place. So, I applied for my master's again—this time, with my whole heart.

I poured every piece of my story into the application for PROPEL (Principal Rapid Orientation and Preparation in Educational Leadership)— a partnership between Florida Atlantic University and Broward Schools that would lead to my master's and assistant principal eligibility.

It was one of the most grueling, vulnerable processes I had ever endured—a timed essay, a panel interview, and the terrifying task of putting my whole heart on display. But I got in.

It felt like more than just an acceptance letter—it felt like a second chance. A cosmic pat on the back that whispered: *You're not done yet*. And just when I thought my heart couldn't hold any more pride, something incredible happened.

In 2019, my Latinos In Action program was honored with **Community Partner of the Year** by Junior Achievement of South Florida. Our students were recognized for their extraordinary commitment to service, leadership, and impact.

It was one of the proudest moments of my career. Not because my name was on the plaque, but because my kids—*our kids*—were seen. Celebrated. Affirmed.

They proved that when young people are given the tools, the space, and someone who believes in them… they can change the world. And me? I finally understood what it meant to turn pain into purpose.

Because here's the truth: I had faced the music. I had named my trauma. I had chosen to stop running and start rewriting. I stopped hiding from the chapters I didn't want to read out loud and started using them as fuel. I didn't just want to survive anymore—I wanted to build something.

Something honest. Something meaningful. Something whole. I had taken my deepest wounds and turned them into wisdom. I had taken my lowest moments and turned them into lessons. And I had begun—truly begun—to rewrite my story.

Still I Stand: A Life Rewritten isn't just a title. It's a promise. It's a declaration. A reminder that no matter how messy the past was, no matter how far you fall, there is always a way forward. And for the first time in a long time… I was finally walking it. Step by step. Breath by breath.

Not chasing perfection. Not erasing the scars. But learning to wear them with grace. Every laugh, every heartbreak, every sleepless night had led me here—to this exact moment—standing on the edge of who I was and who I was still becoming. The path ahead wasn't smooth or certain. It twisted with sharp turns, unexpected storms, and unpromised tomorrows.

But I wasn't afraid anymore. Because I had learned the most important truth of all: you don't need to know exactly where you're going. You just have to trust yourself enough to keep moving.

And so I did.

Chapter Thirteen

From Breakdown to Breakthrough

The master's program was tough, but I was tougher.

Over the next two years, I would earn my master's degree and finally step into the role I had dreamed of for years—assistant principal. But dreams don't manifest without resistance, and this one came with its fair share of detours, doubts, and dark nights of the soul.

During those years of unraveling, I shared a small apartment with a woman I'd met online—Sybil. What started as a practical living arrangement turned into one of the most soulful connections of my life. Sybil was older, though you'd never guess it. Venezuelan. Beautiful. Brilliant. A little wild in the best way. She had an old soul that danced in rhythm with mine. She was loud where I was quiet, fire where I was air. Somehow, she became the sister I hadn't known I needed.

Our memories together could fill a novel. When she became a flight attendant, she took me on my first trip to Europe—and not in coach. First-class. We flew across the Atlantic, wined and dined in Stockholm, and nibbled French baguettes beneath the glittering steel of the Eiffel Tower. We lived like royalty on a budget that didn't make sense, but somehow, we made it work.

But eventually, the party ended.

By then, I could barely afford groceries, let alone rent. I was chasing my dreams with pockets full of lint and a bank account screaming for mercy. Instead of facing the music, I did what I had learned to do far too well—I numbed it. I cracked open my piggy bank, scraped together just enough to buy a 1.5-liter bottle of cheap wine, and drowned out the noise.

Then something strange happened. My phone buzzed. It was my sister, Madeline. She was with Julia. And they were on their way over.

That alone felt like divine intervention. My family rarely visited, and never unannounced. But that night, they came. While Julia filled the room with laughter and small talk—probably chatting with Sybil about food or family or both—I found myself cornered in the best way possible. Madeline looked at me and just... *knew*.

I broke down.

I told her everything. The debt. The fear. The fact that I had drained the last remnants of the trust fund my mother had left me. That despite therapy, despite the job, despite the smile I wore like armor—I was falling apart. The words poured out of me like bricks tumbling from a backpack I had carried too long.

And without hesitation, my family showed up. Again.

That's the thing about us. We don't always answer every call. We go long stretches without visits. We have our baggage. But when someone's on the floor, we show up. We pick them up. Always.

They helped me pay the rent and cover the bills. The next day, Madeline took me grocery shopping, walking with me down each aisle like I was a child learning how to live again. She even helped me find a second job—working security at a local country club. It was humbling, but it was necessary.

And then came the call from my brother, Roberto.

Yes—that Roberto. The one who once told me I'd never succeed if I lived my truth. The one who shattered me in the passenger seat of a 1995 Black Nissan Sentra.

He opened his home to me so I could save money and finish my program. I had to swallow my pride—but I did. And what I found wasn't the cold, judgmental version of him I remembered from years ago. He had changed. Life had changed him. Marriage. Fatherhood. Time. Growth. He had matured.

He hadn't forgotten the promise he made to my mother on her deathbed—to look after me. He honored it. Living with him was healing in a way I didn't expect. He wasn't a man of flowery language, but his actions spoke volumes. He fed me. Housed me. Checked in without hovering.

Before I moved out, we had a moment. He reminded me I wasn't being pushed out—I was being launched. It was time to fly. And then, almost as if it had been sitting on his chest for years, he said something I'll never forget. He told me he admired me. That he'd never met someone like me. That every time I set my sights on something, I made it happen.

And I brought up that moment in the car all those years ago. He had forgotten. I hadn't.

I didn't bring it up to punish him. I wasn't holding a grudge. But I hadn't forgotten the sting of those words—because they had fueled me for years. He apologized. Not in a grand gesture, but in the only way a man like him knows how: with truth. With clarity. He told me he hadn't known better back then. That he was trying to protect me. That he didn't want me to have a hard life in a world that punishes people who dare to live out loud.

But what he didn't realize then—and what I showed him now—was that my light didn't need protection. It needed space to shine. And shine I did. Because people can change. He had. And so had I.

Through this chapter of my life—through my lowest lows and slowest rebuild—I learned something important: the people we write off as villains can sometimes grow into protectors. The same hands that once hurt us can help us heal. People deserve second chances. Just like the one I was given.

Because sometimes, the greatest plot twist isn't who left—it's who came back better. And who you become because of it.

Life isn't just made of second chances. It's made of what we choose to do with them. And when you finally stop running from your pain… you might just run straight into your purpose.

Chapter Fourteen

A Stroke of Bad Luck and Divine Timing

Before I met him, I made a wish.

Not the birthday-candle kind. Not the throw-a-penny-in-a-fountain kind. A quiet, whispered plea to the universe: *Please send me a gay best friend. A GBF.* Someone who got me. Someone who spoke the same language of sarcasm, side-eyes, and shared trauma. Someone who could dance through the chaos with me and remind me that life didn't always have to be so heavy.

And the universe? It delivered.

He was a teacher, like me. A little sarcastic, a lot fabulous. He had just bought a house, and when he offered me a room, I said yes without hesitation. That house became our playground, our refuge, our crash pad after one too many martinis in Wilton Manors.

Let me paint the picture for you: drag queens lip-syncing for their lives. Go-go boys with abs sculpted by the gods—or maybe just good lighting. Watch parties for *RuPaul's Drag Race* where shade was thrown harder than a dodgeball in P.E. And brunches? Honey, bottomless didn't just describe the mimosas—it described our morals on Sunday mornings.

I was living my *best* gay life.

At the same time, I was deep into the PROPEL program—the next step toward becoming an assistant principal. But nothing worth having ever comes easy, right?

Early on, I struggled.

Not because I lacked potential, but because I didn't immediately match what leadership was "supposed" to look like. My clothes were a little too casual. My engagement, a little too quiet. My energy, a little too different. And in a program designed to shape future school leaders, standing out before you're fully formed can feel a lot like standing in the wrong room.

Eventually, they pulled me aside. Told me I might be better suited elsewhere. Offered "alternatives" that felt more like exits than opportunities.

It was all said with a smile, but it sounded an awful lot like what my brother once told me: *You're not going to make it.* And for a moment, I almost believed them both. But I didn't let that stop me. I reflected. Adjusted. I took a long, honest look in the mirror. Then I came back—more focused, more prepared, more determined than ever. Not because I wanted to prove them wrong, but because I wanted to prove to myself that I belonged in every room I walked into.

Then came the pandemic.

Our entire cohort went virtual—because of course it did. The program was already grueling, and now we had to do it from behind a screen, stripped of community and connection. At the time, I was dating someone who, thanks to the shutdown, ended up living with us. Even after we broke up, he stayed. And because my GBF had gotten close to him, he didn't want to kick him out.

That was the lightning before the storm.

The household, once a sanctuary, became suffocating. The lines blurred—between friendship and frustration, between space and suffocation. My mental health started slipping through my fingers again like grains of sand. I was drinking too much. Sleeping too little. Eating like trash. And despite my best efforts, it all started catching up to me.

Then came the day everything caught up at once. I was at work. It started subtly—blurry vision. Not the fun, tipsy kind. Blurred lines. I figured I was just hungover. I chugged water, popped ibuprofen, tried to push through. But it didn't stop. Then my hand went numb. Then my arm. My heart started racing. Something was wrong.

I reached out to a colleague down the hall, who told me to wait until after school to go to the ER. It was 11:30 a.m. But whatever this was… it wasn't going to wait. I called another colleague to escort me to the clinic. Blood pressure? 160 over 120. Heart rate? 110. Still climbing. I called Cassie.

Cassie, like Brenna, had been my ride-or-die since freshman year of high school. A 5'10" blonde goddess with piercing blue eyes and the kind of presence that made people feel both seen and safe. But don't let the goddess aesthetic fool you—she's nerdy, but the sexy kind. Think scrubs and sarcasm, a dash of Hermione Granger, and the confidence of someone who could resuscitate you and roast you in the same breath.

She has a laugh that doesn't just fill a room—it spills into the next one, wraps around you, and reminds you joy still exists. She's a beer snob with a passion for hops and a running enthusiast who once tried to convince me to jog with her. I said no. If you ever see me running, you should run too, because something's gone terribly wrong.

But beyond all that, Cassie is loyalty personified. If she loves you, she's all in. No halfway, no conditions. She'll fight for you. Show up for you. Carry your pain when your legs give out—and still make you laugh through it.

And that day? She didn't just answer the call. When I explained my symptoms, she hung up. Two minutes later, she called back—her voice sharp, urgent. *"You need to get to my ER now, or I'm sending an ambulance."*

My colleague drove me. I called Roberto—my anchor. Calm. Steady. Always. Cassie called again.

"Where are you?"

"Down the block."

"You're showing signs of a stroke. I've prepped your room. The ER Medical Director is on standby."

That was the moment the panic turned real.

We pulled up. Cassie was waiting outside with a wheelchair. *"I can walk,"* I said, rolling my eyes. She leaned in, her tone all business. *"This is my domain, and you will do as I say. Now, get in the damn chair, bitch."*

In my life, I have never been more turned on by a woman. But don't clutch your pearls, y'all—I'm still as gay as a rainbow Speedo at a pool party hosted by Elton John. Stay with me.

She wheeled me in, and the ER team moved fast. Within 30 minutes, I was hooked up to monitors, an IV in my arm, an EKG running, a CT scan ordered. My heart was in A-fib—atrial fibrillation. My heart was beating out of sync, spiking my risk for clots and stroke.

She injected Lovenox, a blood thinner, into my stomach and started meds to slow my heart rate. The devil works hard, but my best friend Cassie? She works harder. Roberto showed up, like he always did, and I finally exhaled.

Then came the diagnosis. A TIA. A Transient Ischemic Attack. A "mini-stroke." Temporary, but deadly if untreated. Had I waited, a major stroke would have followed. I stayed in the hospital for two nights.

The first night, with medication finally quieting my mind, I slept like I hadn't in years.

Cassie saved my life.

And the universe sent a message— gentle, but firm: *Hold on. This isn't how your story ends.* In that stillness, somewhere between the fear and the relief, it settled into my chest. I wasn't just alive. I was being asked to live—with more intention, more fight, more grace than I'd ever believed I had. In the weeks that followed, I stepped back from everything. Work. School. Parties. Pressure. I focused on my health. Got back to the gym. Slowed down.

And then—like a reward for answering the wake-up call—the universe sent me something shiny.

In November, I bought my very own Ford Mustang. A 2019, in a shade best described as "Home Depot Orange," with gloss black rims. It looked better than it sounds. Or maybe it didn't. But I loved it. I had always wanted a Mustang, and now? It was mine.

Some people saw it as a flashy purchase. For me, it was a symbol. Not of material success, but of movement. Of freedom. Of getting back in the driver's seat of my own life.

A month later, in December, I graduated from the PROPEL program. Despite the doubts. Despite the almost-dismissal. Despite the TIA and the stress and the mess—I did it. After years of setbacks, self-sabotage, and stumbling through the dark, I crossed that stage not just as a student, but as someone who had survived himself.

Master's degree: *earned*. Heart: *still beating*. And for the first time in a long time, I wasn't just surviving. I was *becoming*.

But when life forces you to stop—like mine did with a surprise staycation in a hospital gown that barely tied in the back—it doesn't just ask what's next... it asks who's missing from the picture.

It wasn't until years later—after the titles, the breakdowns, the therapy, and the almosts—that I found myself thinking about him again. My brother. We hadn't been close in a long time. Different cities. Different worlds. But when I had my stroke—when life stopped me mid-sentence—I couldn't help but think about the people who shaped me.

He had dropped out of high school. I became a teacher. There's something poetic and painful about that. I spent my career fighting for kids like him—kids who slipped through the cracks because no one ever bothered to look down and pull them back up.

I used to carry guilt for not reaching back sooner. But now, I carry a deeper understanding. Of how trauma splinters people in different ways. Of how survival can look like distance. And how love doesn't always arrive in the ways we expect—sometimes, it's in the quiet ache of who we miss.

My brother may not be part of every chapter in this book, but he's threaded through the margins. In the students I championed. In the kids I mentored. In every young person I refused to give up on.

Maybe that's the legacy we share: two boys who grew up in the same storm. One who got out. And one who taught him why that mattered.

Looking back, this chapter of my life was my "come to Jesus" moment. Not the kind you plan for—more like the kind that shatters you so you can rebuild. It stripped me down to my rawest self, forced me to confront everything I had buried under late nights, cheap vodka, and performative strength.

It was the moment life stopped whispering and started screaming: *"You don't get another chance if you don't take this one!"*

I had been burning the candle at both ends, blind to the fact that I was running on fumes—emotionally, physically, spiritually. And then, in the middle of the chaos I had normalized, my body said *enough*.

It demanded I pay attention.

That I slow down.

That I choose to live.

And so I did.

Because sometimes, the universe doesn't send you signs—it sends you survival. And if you're lucky, it also sends you people like Cassie, like Roberto, like Sybil and Madeline—people who hold you up when you're too tired to stand.

That mini-stroke was a warning, yes—but it was also a gift. A redirection. A divine course correction disguised as disaster.

It forced me to find stillness. To reassess my worth. To remember that my life wasn't just about what I survived, but about what I chose to create in the aftermath. And so I chose... differently.

I chose to heal. I chose to fight for my future. I chose to finish what I started. But the road ahead wasn't easy. Because while the diploma was in my hand, the dream was still dangling just out of reach.

Chapter 15? That's where we find out what happens when you've done the healing, earned the title, and still have to fight like hell to prove you deserve the role you've worked your whole life for.

Hang tight. It's about to get real.

Chapter Fifteen

Grindr, Grit, and Getting the Job

I wasn't looking for anything—or anyone.

After all, I was in my post–mini-stroke glow-up era: healing, rebuilding, keeping my circle small and my martinis cold. But, as the universe tends to do when you finally get your life together, it tossed me a curveball... via Grindr.

For those of you unfamiliar, Grindr is the GPS-powered app where men scroll through torsos like they're shopping for avocados—firm, nearby, and hopefully not too sketchy.

Let me set the scene.

It was a casual night out with my GBF. We were sipping drinks in Wilton Manors—South Florida's version of West Hollywood meets Rainbow Road—and decided to add a little mischief to the evening. A bet was made: the first one to convince a guy from Grindr to meet us at the bar would win. The loser would pay the tab. Simple. Slightly trashy. *Very on brand.*

Thirty minutes later, I had one.

Jordan. Around my height, olive skin, dark brown eyes, long black hair. Sound familiar? Yeah, the universe clearly has a type for me. He was a flight attendant—smart, sarcastic, ambitious, and smooth in conversation. The kind of guy who could hold court with strangers and make it look easy.

We hit it off immediately. Hours passed, drinks flowed, and we shut down the bar like a meet-cute ripped from a pandemic rom-com.

What started as a Grindr game turned into something real. Our dates became more frequent. The chemistry? Undeniable. And on New Year's Eve, at exactly midnight, Jordan asked me to be his boyfriend. I said yes. Cue the glitter, champagne, and slow zoom into our hopeful faces.

But as my relationship bloomed, my friendship with my GBF withered. We started spending less time together, and instead of saying how he felt like a grown adult, he went full soap opera. Passive aggression turned into outright aggression. One night, in a drunken tantrum, he trashed my room—and then denied it the next morning, like gaslighting was an Olympic sport and he was going for gold.

The final straw? He told me he was raising my rent because *"the neighborhood's getting gentrified,"* as if that magically made the utilities more expensive. He wanted to double my rent. Double. For the same room. The same chaos. I'm dramatic, not stupid. I packed my bags and ghosted harder than a hookup who "forgot" to text back.

Plot twist: it was a blessing in the best disguise. Not long after, his life took a sharp detour—complete with headlines, handcuffs, and tabloid tea so messy even I won't spill it. Listen, I love drama as much as the next gay, but not when it comes with an arraignment hearing.

So I moved in with Jordan. We made a home together for the next two years in Wilton Manors.

During that time, I was also doing the most emotionally taxing thing a public educator can do (besides calling parents)—trying to become an assistant principal.

The process? Grueling. Picture this: seven interviews. Each one a panel of four to twelve people, armed with clipboards, forced smiles, and four questions that ranged from student achievement and school safety to how you handle professional development and crises with poise.

You were expected to respond using the STAR method— Situation, Task, Action, Result. Basically, storytelling stripped of tangents, tears, or personality. The first interview? A total flop. I was nervous, too fast, too vague. My anxiety walked in ten minutes before I did.

Thankfully, the director believed in me. She gave me another shot. I returned the next day and crushed it. But still—no offer. Then came the third, fourth, fifth, and sixth interviews. Each time, the feedback was glowing: *"You're doing great… You're polished… You're ready."*

And yet, I kept hearing *"no."*

What most people don't understand is that being an AP isn't just about being qualified. It's about fit. Schools look for leadership styles that match their culture and needs. It's not enough to be capable—you have to be aligned.

Still, I was frustrated. I had worked my ass off. I was ready.

And then—lucky number seven.

On October 6, 2021, I got the call. I was officially being offered a position as an assistant principal at a Title I school I'll call Premier Poverty Preparatory. I cried.

I called my mentors. I called my inner circle. Then I drove straight home to tell Jordan. When I walked in with bottles of champagne, he already knew. We popped them open and ugly-cried together. Because he had seen it all—the disappointments, the rejections—and he had held space for every one of them. He had lifted me up when I doubted myself, and I will always be grateful for that.

Next up: Perla. She and I met when we were colleagues at Monarch High School—she was a counselor, and that alone made me admire her. We would later become best friends.

But Perla isn't just my best friend. She's the kind of soul you thank the universe for, over and over again. The kind who shows up with tequila shots and a calm spirit when your world is spinning too fast. She's equal parts wildflower and wildfire, with a laugh that can light up a funeral and a glare that could shut down Congress.

There's something sacred about our friendship—like the kind you find in novels with dog-eared pages and notes scribbled in the margins. We met when life was still forming me, and somehow, she's stuck around through every version of me—angsty, aimless, ambitious. She never flinched. Never judged. She just held space when I didn't even know I needed it. Perla has this sixth sense—she can detect the exact moment my smile turns into a mask, and she'll rip it right off with either a hug or a sharp word, depending on the day.

She's truth in human form, seasoned with sass. The one I call when I need perspective, prayer, or profanity. The one who reminds me who I am when I start to forget. And if there's one thing I've learned from Perla, it's this: the universe puts people in your life who mirror your soul back to you when the world tries to shatter it.

When I called to tell her the news, she was stranded—car battery dead after picking up her daughter from tennis. So what did I do? I drove to her, surprised her with a rescue ride, and champagne in the trunk. Because friends like Perla? They don't just celebrate you—they crown you. They remind you that you've always been the main character.

Premier Poverty Prep was unlike anything I'd ever seen. It was low-income meets high ambition. Bad and boujee to the core. On my first day, I wasn't welcomed with fanfare or formalities, but with what I would soon learn was the highest form of affection at this school: Cheddar Ruffles, spicy bowls so fiery they should've come with a legal waiver, and fried chicken so good it could make you forget your troubles—and your cholesterol. The smell alone deserved its own welcome committee.

Crockpots were plugged into outlets that probably weren't up to code, plates were passed around like communion, and the side-eye for anyone who dared to skip a plate was downright biblical.

This wasn't just a school—it was a family.

One that fed you, teased you, protected you, and made damn sure you never felt alone. Abbott Elementary had heart, sure. But Premier Poverty Prep? It had heart, hustle, and soul food.

Here, the staff didn't just survive the chaos—they seasoned it, fried it, and served it with a side of sarcasm and sass.

The outgoing principal had retired after 22 years, leaving behind a legacy—and some very high heels to fill. And in her place? The incomparable Latrice Langston.

Picture Olivia Pope from *Scandal*—if she traded crisis management for curriculum mapping and ran a school instead of Washington, D.C. Polished. Brilliant. Unbothered. Powerful. She wore confidence like a designer label and walked the halls like they were her runway.

Her wardrobe? Immaculate. Pencil skirts sharp enough to cut glass, blazers that meant business, and heels that said: *I came to slay and supervise.* Her hair? Always laid. Her nails? Always done. Her presence? Unmistakable.

But it wasn't just her look—it was the way she spoke. With the authority of someone who knew exactly who she was and what she was building. Her words were deliberate, her expectations crystal clear, and when she looked at you, you felt seen—your potential, your flaws, your next ten moves.

She was grace and grit in equal measure. The kind of leader who didn't just manage a school—she commanded it. And under her leadership, I didn't just learn how to be an assistant principal. I learned how to be *that* assistant principal.

Becoming an assistant principal was never just about climbing a ladder for me—it was about becoming the kind of adult I once needed. The kind of person who could see past the chaos of a student's behavior and glimpse the pain—or potential—underneath it.

Sitting behind that desk, wearing that badge, standing at the front of the room during assemblies... it all felt heavier, holier, than I expected. I wasn't just enforcing rules or managing operations. I was shaping lives, one interaction at a time. I was the quiet presence in the hallways, the firm voice in parent meetings, the shoulder students didn't know they needed until they did.

And so much of how I learned to lead—with authenticity, fierce conviction, and the wisdom to know when to listen—I learned from Latrice.

She wasn't just my principal. She was my blueprint. She carried herself with a quiet authority that didn't need to raise its voice to command a room. She had the experience of someone who had seen it all, but the compassion of someone who refused to let cynicism win.

Under her mentorship, I learned that real power wasn't in how loudly you spoke—it was in how you listened. It wasn't in barking orders—it was in setting clear expectations, holding people accountable, and still leaving room for them to grow. She taught me the art of showing up for people on their worst days. That small gestures—an unexpected compliment, a second chance, a well-timed silence—could change the entire trajectory of a student's (or teacher's) day.

Latrice never asked for perfection. What she demanded— without ever needing to say it—was excellence. Integrity. Follow-through. She made me sharper. She made me braver. She made me realize that leadership isn't a title you earn once—it's a choice you make every single day.

Being an assistant principal under Latrice's guidance taught me that leadership isn't about being above others; it's about being beneath them—lifting them higher, steadying them when they stumble, sometimes carrying them until they can walk again on their own.

It wasn't easy. It wasn't glamorous. But it mattered. Because for the first time, I wasn't just surviving—I was building something bigger than myself.

The greatest leaders aren't the ones who demand the spotlight; they're the ones who make sure no one else is left in the dark. And looking back now, I see it for what it truly was: not a finish line, but a beginning. The first steps toward the kind of leader—and the kind of person—I was still becoming.

In retrospect, I realize how rare it is to find a mentor like her— someone who doesn't just sharpen your skills but softens your doubts. Someone who sees not just who you are, but who you could be—and refuses to let you settle for anything less.

I owe so much of the leader—and the person—I became to Latrice. She didn't just shape my career; she helped shape my character.

To this day, she's still one of my biggest cheerleaders—the kind of friend who celebrates my wins louder than I do and reminds me of my worth on the days I forget.

If she ever needed me, I wouldn't just show up—I'd run through a wall for her, no questions asked. Because that's what you do for the people who once did the same for you.

I'm lucky. I didn't just gain a mentor. I gained a lifelong champion and a soul tied to my story forever.

This chapter of my life taught me something I wish more people understood: success is rarely linear. It's a rollercoaster—equal parts thrilling, terrifying, and full of unexpected turns. For every "yes" I celebrated, there were six quiet "no's" I had to fight through. For every title I earned, there were tears shed in silence, battles no one saw, and lessons I had to learn the hard way.

If you take anything from this part of my journey, let it be this: keep showing up. Even when it's hard. Even when the odds feel stacked. Even when the door doesn't open the first, second, or sixth time. Because sometimes, the seventh is where the magic lives.

Believe in your worth. Trust the timing of your story. And remember—every setback is just setting the stage for a comeback.

But as we all know, just when you think you've made it, life throws a plot twist you didn't see coming.

Jordan and I eventually broke up.

The distance between us wasn't loud or cruel—it was quiet, steady, and undeniable. The kind you can't talk your way out of. We tried, of course. We made small adjustments, shared quiet moments, clung to routine. But love—the kind that lasts—needs more than shared memories. It needs momentum. And ours had stalled harder than a Florida A/C in July.

Around the same time, Jordan began to seriously consider moving back to California to be closer to his family. He didn't end up leaving—Florida remained his home. But something between us shifted.

So, we made a choice. We became roommates. And, somehow, better friends than we were lovers. There was no dramatic fight. No explosive ending. Just a mutual understanding that whatever we had— however beautiful and necessary it had been—had run its course.

We let go. With grace. With respect. With gratitude. And to this day, we're still in each other's lives. Because some people come into your life to teach you how to love. Others, to teach you how to let go. Jordan, in his own way, taught me both. But Jordan also gave me something better—in human form. He gave me Stephanie.

I met Stephanie the night Jordan asked me to be his boyfriend on New Year's Eve. From the moment she walked into the room, I was in awe. She had the kind of beauty that turned heads without even trying—but it wasn't just her looks. It was her aura, that unspoken magic she carried. She, too, was Puerto Rican and Dominican, born and raised in New York, and within minutes of meeting her, it felt like I'd known her all my life.

There are people you meet who feel like home. Stephanie was one of them. I remember telling her that night—half-laughing, half-serious—that no matter what happened between Jordan and me, I knew we'd stay friends. And we have. Through every twist, every heartbreak, every new beginning.

She's my first call when I'm craving a wild night out in Wilton Manors, the kind that inevitably ends at New York Grilled Cheese Company at two in the morning. *(If you know, you know.)*

Stephanie is the kind of woman who can turn an ordinary Tuesday into a movie scene. She makes you believe in the goodness of people just by being herself. Her laugh is infectious, her loyalty unshakable, and her soul so pure it reminds you that maybe—just maybe—the world isn't as broken as it sometimes feels. To know her is to love her. To be loved by her is to understand what real friendship looks like—the kind that's loud and messy and golden and real.

Knowing Stephanie was one of those rare gifts life gives you when you're not even looking. But even the brightest connections can't shield you from what's coming next. Because life, in all its divine comedy, has a twisted sense of timing.

Just as I was settling into the rhythm of I've got this, the universe looked down, winked, and said: *"Bet. Hold my beer."*

Right when the love cooled and the dust settled, a storm began to stir—quietly, subtly, and then all at once.

What came next wasn't just a twist. It was a masterclass in humility. In heartbreak. And in how to land when the floor disappears beneath you. Brace yourself.

Chapter Sixteen

The Fall That Taught the Rise

I thought I had *finally* made it.

After seven interviews, months of disappointment, and years of hustle, I had landed my dream role as an assistant principal. I had found my rhythm, my voice, my people. For about eleven months, I poured everything I had into that school—into our students, our staff, our mission. I was building something real, something rooted in purpose and pride. And then... everything changed.

It was late fall. The school year had just begun, and Latrice and I had that campus on lock—like Michelle and Barack co-teaching a masterclass on leadership and legacy. We moved through the halls with the kind of rhythm only true visionaries share—equal parts hope and hustle. We anticipated each other's needs before a word was spoken, finished each other's sentences in meetings, and built systems that didn't just function—they flourished.

Together, we raised expectations, redefined culture, and led that school with purpose, presence, and pride. When we walked into a room, people sat up straighter. We weren't just running a school—we were rewriting its story. Our goal? To make it the premier middle school in our district. And we were doing it—step by step, day by day. You could see it in the students' pride, hear it in the teachers' tone, and feel it in the way people walked the halls like they finally belonged.

Then came the visit. A district leader walked in with the kind of energy that makes the air shift before a single word is spoken. And when they sat us down, the tone said it all before the words did. *"I have to move you."* My heart dropped.

Why? Had I done something wrong? Was this a demotion? No. I was told it was because I had done something right. That my leadership, my skills, and my ability to connect were needed at another school—a larger campus, with a different student population and a new set of challenges.

On paper, it sounded like a promotion. A vote of confidence. A next step. But in my heart? It felt like a gut punch.

Latrice and I had spent the last year building something that was more than systems and spreadsheets. We built trust. Respect. Loyalty. We had each other's backs in a way few colleagues ever do. We spoke the same leadership language. We built momentum between bites of cafeteria mystery meat and hallway huddles that doubled as leadership summits.

We were a team. And now, the team was being split. As soon as the leader left, we both cried—not the quiet, composed kind of cry. The kind that hits your chest and shakes the room. Because in just eleven months, we had become more than coworkers—we had become family. The kind of work family you don't clock out on. Built on sleepless nights, tough conversations, shared victories, and side-eyes that said everything without saying a word.

I've dealt with loss before. I've said goodbye to people I've loved deeply. But this? It's one thing to grieve what's broken—to mourn something that slipped through your fingers because it was already falling apart.

This was different. This felt like mourning something alive. Something thriving. Something just beginning to become everything you'd dreamed it could be.

And I was being asked to walk away—not because I had failed, but because I had done too well. Because my presence was needed elsewhere. Because leadership, as it turns out, often means being pulled from comfort and dropped into chaos. But knowing the why doesn't soften the blow. I was being torn away from a place where I felt seen. Needed. Aligned. From a team that had become family. From a mission that was just beginning to bloom.

This wasn't grief born from loss. This was grief born from love.

And that distinction mattered—more than I realized at the time. Most of my life, I had only known grief as a reaction to devastation: losing my parents—Antonio included. Losing Miles. Losing Lyric. Losing versions of myself I never thought I'd reclaim. I had grieved what was broken, what was taken, what never got the chance to grow. But this? This was the first time I was grieving something beautiful. Something that had worked. Something that had fed my spirit instead of fracturing it.

And that's how I knew I had grown.

Because only someone who has clawed their way out of darkness can recognize the ache that comes from being pulled away from the light. Only someone who's rebuilt themselves from rubble can weep over the loss of something whole.

It meant I had finally found a place that nurtured me. It meant I had become someone worth keeping. And it meant that the love I had poured into that school—into that role—was real. So yeah, this grief was different. Because for the first time in a long time, I wasn't grieving damage. I was grieving joy.

The school I was moved to? The Crucible Academy of Excellence. Before I even started, I tried everything short of smoke signals to reach the principal—emails, phone calls, calendar invites, even a friendly little nudge on LinkedIn. I received no reply. That silence was the first red flag. Looking back, I should've realized then: I wasn't stepping into a new opportunity—I was stepping into a storm.

The moment I walked in, the energy felt off. The atmosphere was so lifeless I half-expected a tumbleweed to roll down the hallway. If my previous school was Disney World—vibrant, purposeful, overflowing with life—this place was Fun Spot America: technically still a theme park, but with knockoff rides, sad mascots, and vibes that whispered *we tried*.

When I finally met the principal, whatever remaining hope I had evaporated. To me, she came across as polished on the outside but fragile beneath the surface—flash on the surface, little substance underneath.

The kind of smile that felt rehearsed; the kind of words that sounded right and landed wrong. My impression was that it was a lot of image and not much depth.

She pulled me in for a hug and launched into a monologue about how she wanted every child in her building to feel loved and supported. Maybe it was genuine, but to my ears it sounded more like a campaign slogan than a conviction. I half-expected a promo code to follow.

Let's just say, her mouth was doing a lot of talking, but sincerity didn't seem part of the conversation.

If I had to compare her to someone, she reminded me of Ava Coleman from *Abbott Elementary*—but without the comedic timing, without the redeeming qualities, and absolutely without the self-awareness. It felt like she was starring in a show no one asked to watch, and still insisted on being the main character.

And me? I was already scanning for the exit.

I considered giving her a name for the sake of the narrative. In the end, I chose not to use one. Some people write themselves out of your story with nothing more than their behavior—and that's how it felt here. I'm not omitting her name out of spite; I'm focusing instead on what this season meant for me.

Regardless of my first impressions, I did what I've always done— I showed up and got to work. I hit the ground running like I'd been there for years, because at the end of the day, I had a job to do. My kids needed me. They were my *why*.

But The Crucible Academy of Excellence wasn't Premier Poverty Prep—and it showed. The job itself wasn't more demanding on paper, but the emotional weight felt heavier. At Premier, I woke up with purpose. At The Crucible Academy, I woke up with knots in my stomach and dread in my chest. Every morning felt like the slow march toward a sentence I didn't deserve—except instead of an orange jumpsuit, I wore business casual. And in my view, she played the role of warden in heels. The kind who, to me, seemed to withhold kindness, weaponize silence, and treat visibility as a threat. I wasn't just navigating a new school—I was surviving a regime.

The one silver lining? It often seemed she was away from campus for off-site commitments at least once or twice a week. The irony, for me, was that while her public messaging leaned inspirational, my experience of the day-to-day was that morale needed life support.

But even in the shadow of her absence—or maybe because of it—I found light. Her office might've felt like a vortex, but the people around me? They were my lifeline. My secretary was, without exaggeration, the kindest, sweetest, most gentle soul I've ever encountered.

She was grace personified—soft-spoken, steady, and warm in a way that made you feel safe just by sitting near her. Her kindness wrapped around you like a hug before she ever said a word, and her presence felt like stepping into a sanctuary. She could calm a storm just by being in the room, and to this day, I carry her warmth with me. She became my compass, my calm in the chaos. She reminded me to eat, forced me to drink water, and could sense when I needed a five-minute breather even before I knew it myself. She was the glue that held me together.

Then there was my brunch crew—a fierce, hilarious, and ride-or-die group that consisted of my assistant principal colleague, our dean, and the internal-suspension teacher. All women. All mothers. All badasses. Our shared language was sarcasm and sass. On tough days, they'd pop into my office with snacks and enough shade to block out the Florida sun. And trust me, they were always on point.

I also shared an office with two other incredible women—our fabulous Guidance Counselor and our whip-smart Literacy Coach. That office became more than a workspace. It was a sanctuary. A therapy room. A war room. A sacred circle of venting and victory. We cried in there. Laughed until we couldn't breathe in there. Rebuilt each other in there.

Funny, isn't it? All women. All mothers. All healers in their own way. And if you've been paying attention, maybe you've noticed the pattern. Because when you grow up without your mother—when that loss leaves a wound that never fully scars over—you start to seek her out in the people you meet. In the kindness of a secretary who keeps M&Ms in her drawer just for you. In the fierce protectiveness of a colleague who says, *"I got you,"* and means it. In the brunch table full of women who refuse to let you drown. I've always been drawn to women like that. Because somewhere deep inside, I'm still that little boy who lost his mom too soon—and the universe, in its quiet grace, keeps placing pieces of her back in my life… one remarkable woman at a time.

To all the remarkable women in my life, this is for you:

For every time you saw my shoulders slump and reminded me to stand tall. For every moment you heard the hesitation in my voice and told me to speak anyway. For every late-night call, every early-morning check-in, every "just making sure you're okay" text that landed right on time—you have been the chorus behind my solo, the grace behind my grit.

You've mothered me in ways that felt like medicine. You've cheered me on when I didn't even believe in myself. You've told me the truth when I needed it—sharp when necessary, soft when it mattered most. You have shown up with coffee, wine, hugs, laughter, leftovers, affirmations, brutal honesty, unconditional love—and more often than not, all at once.

You've reminded me what resilience looks like when worn with lipstick and hoop earrings. You've modeled leadership in stilettos and fire in your eyes. You've carried burdens I'll never fully understand and still made space to carry mine. You are the reason I'm still standing.

So if you've ever dried my tears, made me laugh when I wanted to disappear, fought for me in rooms I wasn't in, or simply said, "I'm proud of you"—thank you. Thank you for choosing me. For loving me. For lifting me. You are the backbone of this story.

I hope you see yourself in these pages. Because you were there all along.

With love,

—Chris

Despite the warriors of women I had by my side—who lifted me, anchored me, and reminded me of my worth on the darkest days—I made one crucial mistake: I underestimated what I was up against.

In my second year at The Crucible Academy, things went from bearable to brutal. The shift was slow at first, almost imperceptible, like a crack spreading in glass. I received a strong performance review for the previous year praising my leadership, initiative, and campus impact. It was one of those reviews that affirms you're in the right place, doing the right work.

Within a couple of weeks, I was surprised with an informal write-up. Then another the following month. And another after that. Each one chipped away at my confidence, my credibility, and ultimately, my spirit. By the time the school year neared its end, I received a formal write-up that would live in my permanent record like a stain I couldn't scrub off.

Now listen—I'm not perfect. I take responsibility for the things I did mess up: missed deadlines, minor operational hiccups, some communication lapses. But the way it felt, every small mistake was documented and magnified. I didn't experience it as accountability but as ammunition. To me, it seemed less about helping me improve and more about building a case.

It felt like I had a target on my back. I was drowning—not in incompetence, but in what I experienced as cruelty. And instead of throwing me a lifeline, it felt like she stood by, watching me sink. In my darkest moments, I even imagined her smiling.

And the cruelest part? I would later learn the root cause of the misery I was enduring. It wasn't just about missed deadlines or operational errors. No. It was betrayal—from within.

I had trusted the wrong people, said the wrong things to the wrong ears. People I considered colleagues—or worse, friends— repeated my private frustrations, and I felt like those words were used against me. As the saying goes: if you can't handle criticism, you can't handle growth. But here's what I'll add: if you're not open to growth, criticism can feel less like a mirror and more like a weapon.

Then came the moment I'll never forget—the moment that cracked something in me so deeply, I can still feel the tremors.

It was a quiet Friday afternoon before a long weekend. The school was quiet, half-empty, coasting toward the long weekend. She summoned me to her office. Nothing unusual—until I saw who was sitting beside her. Her secretary. My work mom. Yet another woman who offered calm in chaos and tucked quiet encouragement into the folds of the hardest days. She couldn't even look me in the eye. Her hands trembled. Her silence screamed.

My gut twisted. I sat down, breath shallow, heartbeat in my ears. And then she said it: *"We will not be renewing your contract as assistant principal."* My ears burned. The air thickened. I blinked, waiting for the punchline. There wasn't one. She laid out my options like it was some kind of negotiation: *demotion... or resignation.*

My throat tightened. I wanted to scream. I wanted to flip the desk. I wanted to tear away the mask I believed she'd worn for two years and shout, *"This is who you really are!"* I wanted to ask what kind of leader preaches love and support while pulling the rug out from under someone trying to survive.

But more than anything, I wanted to cry. Not from weakness, but from rage. From disbelief. From the gut-punch of realizing I was being discarded like a plotline that no longer served someone else's narrative. My contract wasn't just terminated—it felt like someone else was trying to write the end of my story. But what she didn't know? I've rewritten chapters before. And I wasn't done.

I walked out of her office in a daze—numb, disoriented, like I'd been hit by a car but couldn't find the bruises yet. My body kept moving, but my mind hovered somewhere above, struggling to make sense of how everything I'd built had collapsed in a single sentence.

And then came the cherry on top of the betrayal sundae. The following week, she strutted into my office, wearing a smile so bright it could've lit up Times Square, and announced that she had received a promotion. *A promotion.* She wouldn't be the principal at The Crucible Academy anymore. She was moving on—to a bigger title, a bigger paycheck, a new building, a fresh start. Meanwhile, I stood in the rubble of what I thought was my future.

Hearing her say it—so casually, like she was talking about brunch plans—felt like a slap across the face. Insult on top of injury. Rage, which had been simmering quietly beneath the sadness and confusion, erupted.

I pleaded. I swallowed my pride and asked her to reconsider. After all, if I was no longer under her leadership, what was the point of going through with it? Why torch my career if I was no longer her "problem"?

I received a standard reply about "decisions being final" and "wishing me the best moving forward"—the kind of politeness that made it clear I'd already been filed away. The door didn't just close—it slammed, hard enough to knock me off my feet.

And just like that, the damage was done. Permanent. Personal. Irreversible. This wasn't just a professional setback. This was a punch to the soul. This was betrayal dressed up in bureaucracy, cruelty disguised as protocol.

Because it was never just about the title. It was about everything I had poured into that role. The late nights. The early mornings. The weekends. The missed birthdays. The emotional labor. The belief that I was doing something that mattered. That I was changing lives. But this decision made it feel like none of it counted.

And that kind of grief? It sticks to your ribs. It doesn't come with flowers or sympathy cards. It doesn't scream. It whispers, *"You weren't good enough."*

But I've heard that whisper before. In classrooms where I was overlooked. In homes where my queerness was unspoken. In relationships where love was conditional. In memories that echo with absence.

And every single time, I've answered back—louder. With grit in my voice. With purpose in my step.

With the kind of unshakable resolve that only comes from surviving what was meant to break you.

Life has tried to chew me up and spit me out. But I'm built like a piece of corn—tough, stubborn, and impossible to crush. You can toss me around, strip me bare, but I'll still hold onto the sweetness inside. That's the thing about people like me: we don't just survive. We keep showing up. Again and again. No matter how many times the world tries to grind us down.

I've taken their doubt, their dismissal, their whispered attempts to dim my light—and I've turned it into fuel. Because every setback, every closed-door conversation, every underestimation... I've met it with a rise.

Louder. Bolder. Unapologetically me.

So I sat with the ache. I let it burn. Because I knew—on the other side of this pain was clarity. Strength. Purpose.

That door may have slammed behind me, but it didn't define my exit. I didn't leave broken. I left armed—with keys forged from truth, from hard lessons, from harder love, from voices that whispered, *"Keep going."*

Chapter Seventeen

Friendships and Fresh Starts

When I walked away from her office that day, it felt like everything I had built was unraveling. The title was gone. The office stripped. The badge, the nameplate—symbols of a role I had poured myself into—reduced to memories and HR paperwork. But here's what she couldn't take: my purpose. My calling. My why. Leadership hadn't left me. It had simply shifted.

And in the quiet aftermath, as the dust of heartbreak settled and the bruises of betrayal began to fade, something unexpected began to bloom again inside me: *hope.* Hope that maybe returning to the classroom wasn't a step back—but a step closer to what really mattered.

I had spent years climbing ladders, chasing titles, proving my worth in boardrooms and leadership meetings. But maybe—just maybe—it was time to return to the place where I first found myself: the classroom. The heartbeat of the school. The front lines of change.

Because while the world sees teaching as a job, I know better. Teaching is a revolution in motion. It's showing up every day to spark minds, to mend spirits, to fight battles no one else sees—and to remind young people that they matter. That their stories matter. That they are not invisible.

So, I brushed off the dust, took a deep breath, and opened a new door—one with the familiar creak of desks, the scratch of pencils on paper, and the quiet hum of possibility in every student's gaze.

This wasn't the end. It was my beginning… again. And this time, I wasn't walking in to prove anything. I was walking in to teach—and to feel everything again.

Because sometimes, when the world strips you down to your barest truth, that's when you remember who you are. And I was always… *a teacher.*

After the school year ended, I wandered through the summer like a balloon that had slipped from a child's hand—weightless, directionless, slowly drifting. I wasn't tethered to a school, a purpose, a title. And for someone like me—someone who thrived in the hustle, who breathed through the rhythm of structure and responsibility—that kind of freedom felt more like a void.

But that summer, a few unexpected things became my saving grace. First, my four-legged therapist in a fur coat: Milo.

Jordan had gifted him to me two years earlier for my birthday. We rescued him from Big Dog Ranch Rescue in Palm Beach County, the largest cage-free, no-kill rescue in the country. His original name? Santorini. Yes, like the Greek island. Fancy, right? He came pre-packaged like a dog from a resort brochure. All he was missing was a cocktail and a pair of sunglasses.

His mom, a purebred chocolate Lab, was also at the rescue—but Milo looked like she might've had a little fling with the neighborhood boxer. And possibly a pit bull. He grew to her size, but with a face full of character: sleek black fur, a white-speckled undercoat, and a patchwork quilt of scrappy charm and muscle. He looked like he could break down a door but preferred to break hearts instead.

Around others, he had the energy of a frat boy at an open bar—leaping, licking, vibrating with joy. But at home, with just me? He was a teddy bear in a powerlifter's body. Quiet. Gentle. Loyal. And somehow, he knew. He knew I was going through it. He'd press his head into my chest when I cried. Lick the tears off my cheeks with quiet purpose. Curl up at my feet like he was guarding not just my body, but my spirit.

Of course, let's not forget his love affair with destruction.

He didn't bark. He didn't bite. Unless, of course, you count chewing through my vertical blinds, baseboards, dog beds, and—his personal favorite—my most expensive shoes. That phase? Oh, it was a real treat. Nothing says character building like coming home to a living room that looks like a crime scene sponsored by Chewy.com.

But here's the truth: Milo got me out of bed when nothing else could. When my thoughts were too heavy and my grief felt too sharp, he was the one thing that needed me. And needing him gave me purpose.

Science backs it up, too. Studies show that dogs help lower cortisol, increase serotonin, and reduce symptoms of anxiety and depression.

But you don't need a study to know dogs are good for the soul—not when you're being licked awake at 9:00 a.m. by a 70-pound furball whose only agenda is love, fresh air, and maybe a squirrel chase or two.

Forget the science and the cortisol charts; when Milo jumped on my bed, tail thumping like a drumline and tongue flopping across my face like it was covered in peanut butter, I didn't need a research paper to feel better—I was already healing.

Therapy's great, but so is being dragged out of bed by a dog who treats every walk like a sacred mission and reminds you, in his own ridiculous, joyful way, that the world is still worth showing up for.

He didn't just save me. He grounded me.

And then, there was Greece.

A trip I had planned long before I knew the bottom would fall out of my professional life. Call it fate. Call it divine timing. But it felt like the universe had pre-booked this healing on my behalf.

Two weeks. Eight days and seven nights aboard the Virgin Voyages Resilient Lady, setting sail out of Athens and docking in Santorini, Rhodes, Bodrum, and the party mecca of Mykonos. Greece wasn't just a trip. It was a baptism by saltwater and sunlight.

I partied in Mykonos until the sun came up over whitewashed rooftops and blue domes. I danced on cobblestone streets with strangers who became friends and drank cocktails made by a Greek bartender who looked like he'd stepped out of a myth. Tattooed, brooding, that smirk... and his voice? Melted me faster than feta in the Aegean sun. Sure, he was straight—but in my fantasy, he was my "Greek boyfriend," and you know what? A boy can dream.

I even googled how to move there. I pictured myself sipping

espresso on a terrace overlooking the sea, writing by day, teaching online by night. For a minute, I believed I might never go back. But dreams have alarms, and eventually, they ring. And sometimes? They come with trophies.

In my two years at The Crucible Academy of Excellence, I became deeply involved with both the school and county's PTA—thanks in large part to two extraordinary moms, Amy and Samira, who didn't just run their PTA chapter, they lived it. Their conviction, their hustle, and their love for kids was unmatched. They made advocacy look like a superpower. And I showed up—for every meeting, every fundraiser, every initiative—because they inspired me to.

At first, I thought Amy was an entitled...

Brassy,

Insufferable,

Temperamental,

Condescending,

Holier-than-thou type.

The kind who shows up to meetings in oversized sunglasses, an iced latte in one hand and judgment in the other.

But once I broke through that perfectly curated exterior, I discovered the truth: she's still a *bit*... much—but she's also fiercely loyal, whip-smart, and has a selfless soul for the people she lets into her orbit. And somehow, I became one of them. Amy doesn't do fake. She doesn't do passive. She's a force—a sharp tongue with soft edges when it matters most. She grew to love me like one of her own, and I never took that lightly.

And then there's Samira. She is strikingly beautiful, inside and out—graceful, grounded, and a pillar of quiet strength. Her faith is part of that strength, something she carries with dignity and grace. She has the patience of a saint and the quiet power to turn a school cafeteria into a gala—with poise, purpose, a clipboard, and a smile. Samira walks into a room and instantly brings peace, but don't mistake that for weakness. She's the kind of woman who will advocate, uplift, and fight for what's right—with precision, poise, and a quiet fire that commands respect.

Together, they were my PTA dream team. But more than that—they were my people. They reminded me that you don't need a title to lead, and that sometimes, the fiercest warriors in education aren't in classrooms or offices... they're in carpool lines and volunteer spreadsheets, rewriting the rules and raising the bar for what it means to show up.

Through their encouragement (and let's be honest, a few gentle shoves), I went on to serve on the Broward County Council of PTA/PTSAs as the LGBTQIA+ Chair, ensuring representation for students and families who needed it most. And that summer, in the middle of heartbreak and healing, I was honored with a moment of breathtaking irony: I was named **Florida PTA's Outstanding Administrator of the Year**.

Yeah. That happened. It was poetic. It was healing. It was one of the most validating moments of my life—standing on that stage, accepting an honor that didn't just recognize what I had done, but who I was: a leader, an advocate, and a fighter for what's right. And just when I thought it couldn't get better, it did.

I would later go on to receive the **Florida Panthers' ¡Vamos Gatos! Hispanic Excellence Award**, honoring individuals of Hispanic heritage who make outstanding contributions to their communities. The nomination? It came from one of my warrior women colleagues—proof that even in your lowest seasons, people are watching… and rooting for you.

Two awards in one year. One from the people who saw me rebuild. One from the culture that raised me. Both from the community that never gave up on me.

It was the universe, once again, whispering—and this time shouting: *"They tried to write you off. But we wrote you back in."*

When I returned from Greece, my birthday was fast approaching, but I didn't feel like I had a reason to celebrate. The sting of that recent chapter still clung to my skin. But my friends wouldn't let me wallow. They called, they texted, they reminded me of something I had forgotten—I was still loved. I was still surrounded. I was still standing.

So, I planned a dinner at one of my favorite restaurants. Nothing extravagant. Just dinner. Connection. Presence. And when the day came, they showed up—every single one of them. Most of them were my warrior women and their husbands, dressed up, smiles wide, hearts open.

We shared a meal. We laughed like we had been storing it up for months. And at the end of the night, I did what I've always done—I gave a speech. I looked each of them in the eye and thanked them, individually, with a story or memory that captured exactly why they meant so much to me.

Because for all that I had lost that year, I hadn't lost sight of this: the power of people who show up for you. And then Perla stood up. With tears in her eyes, she said, *"Chris has brought together a dynamic and diverse group of people, and knowing him, we know how much he exudes so much goodness. We all know his plight, and what he's been through. And still, he continues to shine his light. And the first thing he did, on his birthday, was celebrate us. His people."*

She didn't need to say the words "Keep writing. Keep going." She lived them in her speech. In the way she reminded me—reminded all of us—that this story isn't over. That this pain isn't pointless. That this heart of mine still had chapters to write.

And in that moment, as low as I had been feeling, I was reminded of the friend I am. The kind who, even on his worst day, will find a way to honor the people who carried him. The kind who doesn't just survive—but gives thanks along the way.

Because that's who I've always tried to be. No matter how far I go, how much I achieve, or how deeply I fall—I never forget the hands that held me. The people who showed up. The ones who kept the light on.

And that night? That room full of love and laughter? That was proof that I may have been broken… but I was never alone.

It also reminded me of something deeper—something this entire journey has echoed again and again: friendships aren't background characters in our stories. They're the lifelines. The mirrors. The medicine. They're the laughter in the hospital room, the midnight text when the weight gets too heavy, the celebration when you've forgotten how to celebrate yourself.

In every chapter of my life—through heartbreak, healing, triumph, and trauma—my friends have been the common thread. They've helped stitch me back together with grace, grit, and a little glitter when needed.

Now, if you ask my family or even some of my friends, they'll tell you I have too many best friends. Like, "Are you starting a fan club?" levels of best friends. The running joke is that I hand out the title like I'm hosting the Best Friend Olympics and everyone gets a medal. And honestly? They're not wrong.

But let's get one thing straight: I don't use the term "best friend" lightly. It's not just a cute label for someone I had brunch with twice. My best friends have been through it with me. They've witnessed the mess, the magic, and the meltdowns. They've seen me at my lowest—on the bathroom floor, a bottle of wine deep, wondering if I'm still enough— and somehow managed to remind me that I was. They've dropped everything to sit with me in silence. Talked me off ledges I built with my own insecurities. Clapped for me when I had nothing left but tears—and still showed up, lipstick on, ready to fight for my joy.

So yeah, maybe I've got a small army of best friends. But each one reflects a different part of me back to myself—the version who's soft but strong, messy but magical, broken but still building. And if you think that's "too many," then maybe you've never been loved by a tribe that lifts you the way mine does.

And while we're on the subject of best friends—let me tell you about a few more who carved out space in my heart during one of the most intense chapters of my life. First up: Alysha and Althea.

We met in the trenches of the PROPEL program, but it wasn't just academic stress and leadership aspirations that bonded us. We were three New Yorkers—bold, fast-talking, sarcastic as hell—and underneath all that: three people who knew what it meant to hustle for a dream while carrying the weight of our personal lives.

They were both single moms raising sons, showing up with strength, grace, and lashes that could cut glass. They felt like sisters—bound not by blood, but by a shared fire. A tenacity. A hunger to rise, not just for ourselves, but for the kids and communities we represented.

We carried each other through the hardest parts of the program—through research papers that nearly broke us, late-night encouragement texts, voice notes full of laughter, and group projects that tested everything but our friendship. They held me up when I doubted myself, and I did the same for them. We weren't just earning degrees—we were becoming the kind of leaders we had once needed. And we did it together. They reminded me that sometimes, your chosen family finds you exactly when you need them most.

And that brings me to the glamorous, glorious reveal of yet another best friend (yes, *another one*—my therapist calls it a support system; I call it my personal board of directors). Her name? Kamille. She's been my ride-or-die since high school—22 years and counting.

If Prince Eric and Tiana had a baby, hired Oprah as her life coach, and raised her on Disney magic, coconut oil, and herbal self-care, it'd be Kamille in all her caramel-skinned, crown-wearing glory. Her skin deserves its own filter, her cheekbones could cut tension, and her presence? Sculpted by the gods and told, *"Now go be extra."*

She's like champagne—fizzy, loud, and best served with a warning label. She'll light up a room with one laugh, but cross her, and that sparkle? It turns into a four-alarm wildfire faster than you can say, *"Hold my earrings."* Her heart's made of 24-karat gold… but baby, the fire is real.

In June 2023, I had the honor of officiating her wedding—a moment that meant the world to me. Because it wasn't just a ceremony. It was a full-circle moment. We've walked through every season of life together—from late-night phone calls about our relationships to grown-up talks about marriage, motherhood, and mortality. Standing beside her as she married the love of her life was more than symbolic—it was sacred. It reminded me how far we've come, how much we've survived.

And speaking of survival, Kamille recently kicked cancer's ass like the boss she is. She did it with grace, grit, and a sense of humor sharp enough to make the chemo machines flinch. She's also now the proud mother of a beautiful baby boy who's already showing signs of inheriting her sass, her strength, and her soft skin.

So, yeah. Another best friend. Another miracle in human form.

Together, Brenna, Cassie, and Kamille are like real-life Charlie's Angels—if Charlie were a gay man with abandonment issues, a group chat that could be subpoenaed for emotional evidence, and an unhealthy dependency on brunch. One's the firecracker, one's the softie with a scalpel for truth, and one's the glamazon who could smite you with a smile. And me? I'm just grateful they keep showing up for the mission—heels on, hoops in, and hearts wide open.

In October 2022, Cassie got married—to a woman named Ryanne, and let me tell you, it was the gayest, most glorious wedding I've ever attended—and I loved every glitter-soaked, champagne-fueled minute of it.

Five days in Key West. A beach wedding that looked like it was scripted by the Hallmark Channel but with better outfits. A Sunday Funday water adventure that included bottomless drinks, drag queen energy, and enough sunburns to qualify for a worker's comp claim. A time was had.

Being Cassie's Best Man wasn't just an honor—it was another full-circle moment. Their union didn't just solidify my friendship with Cassie; it gifted me a bonus best friend in Ryanne—a Pokémon-loving, quick-witted, charming hurricane of joy who fit into our circle like she'd been there all along.

Where Cassie is steady, Ryanne is spark. Where Cassie thinks deeply, Ryanne cracks the joke that breaks the tension. Together, they didn't just build a marriage—they expanded our family. And somehow, the adventure just keeps getting better.

Because these aren't just best friends. These are soul mirrors. Lifelines. People who walk into your story when the plot twists get dark—and refuse to leave until the light returns.

So if you take anything from this memoir, let it be this: nurture your friendships like sacred ground. Protect them. Show up for them. Speak your love out loud, often. Don't wait for birthdays or breakdowns to say thank you.

Because in the end, it's not the titles or milestones or Instagrammable moments that define a life well lived—it's the people who walked with you through the mess, danced with you in the joy, and said, *"I see you. I've got you. I'm here."* That… is everything.

And if you're my best friend and you're reading this, you need to know this isn't just a thank you. It's a sacred acknowledgment. You are inked into these pages not as a character, but as the heartbeat of my healing. You've changed my life in ways I'll never be able to repay.

Every time I say "best friend," I mean you. I mean your name, your laughter, your loyalty. You didn't just show up. You stayed. And because of that—I'm still here.

Still writing.

Still rising.

Still standing.

Chapter Eighteen

Back to the Board—Where the Comeback Began

They say rock bottom teaches you lessons that mountaintops never will. But what they don't always say is that the climb back up starts with something as simple—and as profound—as a voice on the other end of the line.

This next chapter is about the rise. The reset. The return. And not just in my career—but in my health, my habits, and my relationship with myself.

After Greece—and the whirlwind of cocktails, late nights, and that glorious "birthday bender"—I came home thinking I could just shake it all off. But my body had other plans. At my annual physical, my doctor didn't bother with soft landings. *"Your blood pressure is elevated. Your cholesterol is high. Liver enzymes? Concerning. And Chris... you're pre-diabetic."* Well, happy belated birthday to me.

She recommended a weight-loss medication called Zepbound, similar to Ozempic, but better suited to address the issues piling up. I'll be honest—I resisted. It felt like cheating. Like I was taking the "easy way out." But she wasn't offering a shortcut—she was handing me a lifeline. And something inside me, tired of carrying the weight in every possible way, finally said yes.

I committed. I joined a gym—and went. I meal-prepped like it was a religion. I made every bite matter instead of just counting calories. I drastically cut back on drinking—because spoiler alert: vodka doesn't fix sadness; it just prolongs the crash. And slowly, week by week, my body responded. In five months, I lost 40 pounds. My bloodwork? Nearly perfect.

But the best part? I started to feel like me again. Not the broken version riddled with rejection and burnout—but the version who knew how to fight for a future. This wasn't about a number on a scale. It was about honoring the body that carried me through trauma, grief, and survival—and finally treating it like it deserved to thrive.

Because healing isn't just emotional. Sometimes, it's physical. And this time, I wasn't chasing perfection. I was chasing peace.

Then, after all the falling, the grieving, the rebuilding—I got the call. It was from the district. And just like that, the waiting was over. I was no longer suspended in limbo. I had been assigned to a new school.

The first time their number popped up on my phone, I just stared at the screen. It felt like it might bite. Answering meant opening a door I wasn't sure I had the courage to walk through again. But I did. Slowly. Cautiously.

"Hi, is this Christopher Machado?" The voice on the other end was warm. Steady. Present.

"Yes, speaking."

"Hello, this is Ms. Williams-DeVyne… did you get a very exciting email today? Because we are so excited to have you join our family." Her tone wasn't

robotic or rehearsed. It was real. And after months of cold silences, clipped emails, and forced niceties—her sincerity hit me like a sunbeam breaking through after a long, gray storm.

It was the first time in a long time someone sounded genuinely happy to have me. Not because of what I'd accomplished. Not because of what I could do for school grades or metrics. But because of who I was. Ms. Williams-DeVyne spoke like someone who already saw value in me before I even stepped foot in her building. And that? That mattered. That made me feel welcome in a way I hadn't felt in months.

In that moment, I realized this wasn't just a placement. It was a promise. A whisper from the universe that said, *"You're not finished yet."* I wasn't just being given a new assignment. I was being handed a new chapter.

To rise. To rebuild. To return to the front lines—where I've always belonged. And this time? I wasn't walking in with wounds. I was walking in with wisdom.

Bare Minimum Magnet Middle School.

Don't let the name fool you—it's as ironic as it is accurate. Yes, the building had seen better days. Yes, resources were tight and the challenges were stacked. But beneath the chipped paint and outdated tech was something no school report could ever quantify: *soul*.

This was a true community school. The kind of place where teachers kept extra granola bars in their desks because they knew who was coming to school hungry. Where staff quietly pitched in for uniforms. Where birthdays were remembered, hugs were currency, and grace was extended daily.

The teachers here didn't just clock in. They showed up. For their kids. For each other. For a mission bigger than themselves. Many had stayed through leadership turnover, budget cuts, and the ever-changing demands of the district.

Why? Because they believed in their students. Because they knew that sometimes, the kids who act out the most are the ones who need love the loudest. This wasn't a school that had given up—it was a school that refused to be given up on.

So while the nickname might've been a little shady shorthand among those in the know, the truth was anything but minimal. What I found there was grit. Passion. Loyalty. Educators who poured themselves into kids who'd been counted out far too many times. And that? That was the kind of place I was proud to be assigned to. The kind of place that felt like it just might become home.

And at the helm of it all was a woman who didn't just lead—she lifted. Ms. Williams-DeVyne, the principal of Bare Minimum Magnet, was nothing like what I'd just escaped. From our very first phone call, her voice carried a warmth I hadn't realized I'd been longing to hear. And she meant it. Every word.

She wasn't flashy or performative. She didn't pretend to have all the answers. But what she did have was heart. Real heart. A leadership style rooted in trust, compassion, and an unshakable belief in the power of second chances—for kids, for teachers... for people like me.

She saw me before she ever met me. Welcomed me before I even walked through the door. And that kind of welcome, after everything I had just endured, wasn't just refreshing—it was redemptive. But here's where the story starts to shift. My first introduction to the staff was anything but ordinary.

Instead of a standard meet-and-greet in the media center with stale coffee and grocery-store bagels, Ms. Williams-DeVyne arranged a welcome-back breakfast at a soul food restaurant just blocks from campus. A bold choice. A beautiful one. And deeply telling of the kind of leader she was.

That morning, I was anxious. New setting, fresh scars, unsure of how I'd be received in a school where no one yet knew my story. But the second I stepped inside, the nerves began to melt. The aroma of biscuits and gravy met me at the door, and so did she—Ms. Williams-DeVyne. She greeted me with the same warmth and authenticity I'd heard in her voice. She wasn't just smiling—she was glad I was there. You could feel it. And that? That made all the difference.

She had a presence about her that didn't need to announce itself—strong, compassionate, calm under pressure. The kind of leader who could quiet a room without raising her voice. The kind who knew her staff's birthdays and their breaking points. She didn't just run a school—she carried it. On her back. With love.

I sat down at a table, still cautiously optimistic, and was immediately welcomed by staff I'd never met. Their faces were full of curiosity—not the kind that's nosy, but the kind that's hopeful. They didn't know what I'd been through. They didn't know the chapter I was walking away from. But they were happy I was there. And sometimes, that's enough to start again.

Then she walked in—Ms. Waverly-Banks. The name sounded like she ran a luxury law firm. She looked like she'd stepped off a glossy magazine cover. And she moved through the room with the quiet confidence of someone who had seen a thing or two and come out stronger for it. I fell in love instantly. Imagine that—another woman.

Ms. Waverly-Banks would go on to become my immediate supervisor, overseeing my department, but more importantly—she became my partner in leadership. We didn't just share responsibilities— we shared vision, purpose, and the drive to transform our students' outcomes. And from the very beginning, I knew: this was a woman who wasn't here to play. She was here to build.

Two weeks into the school year, the school's Literacy Department Chair suddenly resigned. Without hesitation, I submitted my name for the role. It wasn't about the title—it was about the mission.

Our school grade was within reach of a higher designation. Close enough to taste. All we needed was a little momentum. A little structure. A little fight. And I had all three. I had learned from my last school—*oh, I had learned*. No distractions. No politics. No stepping outside my role. This time, I stayed in my lane. And I floored it.

Setting up my classroom again after years in administration felt... *sacred*. There was something almost poetic about unboxing dry erase markers instead of data binders. About rearranging desks instead of meeting agendas. For the first time in what felt like forever, I wasn't preparing for walkthroughs or evaluations—I was preparing for kids. Real kids. With real stories. And suddenly, everything felt real again. This wasn't just a classroom. It was a safe haven. A sanctuary in cinder blocks. My little 8th-grade oasis.

The moment students walked in, I wanted them to feel it. The LED lights glowed soft and inviting—not that blinding institutional white that makes you feel like you're walking into an operating room. Music played in the background—sometimes lo-fi beats, sometimes Beyoncé, depending on the mood (and the morning). Posters with affirmations covered the walls. Quotes from authors. A "Wall of Wins." A corner with books, pillows, and permission to just be.

And then, there was me. Not the assistant principal. Not the polished panel interview candidate. But the teacher. Raw. Ready. And rooted. I wasn't just teaching standards—I was building confidence, cultivating curiosity, and reminding every student who sat in my classroom that their voice mattered. That their story mattered. That they didn't have to shrink to fit into anyone's rubric.

They were walking into a space where they wouldn't just learn about central themes and textual evidence—they'd learn about themselves. And I showed up every day not to hand them success on a silver platter… but to wrap it up in a metaphor, tie it with a simile, and deliver it like the plot twist they never saw coming.

Because that's what teaching is. It's storytelling. It's stagecraft. It's survival. And in that classroom, I was home again.

But as much as the classroom gave me purpose, it was the

people— the unexpected connections—that gave me peace. And one of those people? Ms. Jasmine Peña, the principal's secretary.

There are some people you meet, and instantly—no explanation needed, no small talk required—your souls just click. That was the feeling I got the moment I met Jasmine. We were around the same age, which made it easy to connect, but it was more than that.

If Jennifer Lopez never made it to stardom and instead decided to run the heartbeat of a public middle school, that would be Jasmine— glamorous, grounded, and drop-dead stunning. She had that Bronx-born sparkle (even though she wasn't from the Bronx) and a work ethic that could humble most CEOs.

Jasmine was the glue that held the school together. The kind of person who knew how to juggle twenty things at once—copy machine crises, lunch deliveries, parent phone calls—and still managed to look flawless doing it. She was equal parts administrative wizard and resident vibe curator.

A ray of sunshine on a rainy day, with just enough sass to keep things interesting. And me? I became a permanent fixture in her office. Not because I had endless clerical needs (though middle school teaching will give you plenty), but because being around Jasmine was like taking a deep breath.

She was my daily escape—my quick coffee break without the caffeine, my midday exhale. We'd talk life, laugh at the madness of the day, and remind each other to keep showing up—unhinged but heartfelt, slightly chaotic but still caring.

Jasmine wasn't just a secretary. She was another lifeline. A safe space. A reminder that, even in the chaos, there's always someone who gets it—and gets you.

The kids were a mix of everything I loved about middle school—awkward, brilliant, hilarious, vulnerable, and full of possibility. Some had walls so high you had to scale them with patience. Others walked in ready to tell you about their weekend like you were a long-lost cousin. But all of them? They needed love. They needed structure. And they needed someone to see past the essays and eye rolls to the aching, beautiful, complicated humans beneath. And that? That was my specialty.

Before the first bell even rang that year, I knew something deep in my bones: this was going to be the best year of my teaching career yet. Why? Because I was walking in as the kind of teacher forged in fire.

I wasn't new to the classroom—I had found my purpose there once before. But this time, I wasn't just returning with lesson plans and anchor charts. I was returning with battle scars. With wisdom. With a sharpened sense of who I was and what I was there to do.

I had taught before I ever wore a tie and carried a walkie-talkie. And I had led—with love and high standards—through the chaos of Title I realities, staffing shortages, emotional breakdowns, and administrative red tape. As an assistant principal, I saw it all. The magic and the mess. The teachers who changed lives. The ones who phoned it in. The ones who were burning out right in front of me. The ones who, even with empty tanks, still showed up every day because they believed in this work. I learned from all of them. And when I came back to the classroom, I carried those lessons with me.

I was the kind of teacher who knew how to meet a student where they were without ever lowering the bar. Who believed that structure and love were not opposites—but partners. Who greeted students by name, noticed new haircuts, clocked silent pain, and knew when a bathroom break was really a cry for help.

I was the kind of teacher who taught standards, yes—but wove in stories and real-world connections that made my classroom feel like something between a TED Talk, a therapy session, and a comedy special.

I taught with rigor. With heart. With rhythm. Because I had lived through the heartbreak of leadership—and now I was leading from the heart.

All those years as an administrator didn't distance me from the work. They brought me closer to it. They helped me see what good teaching looked like. What great teaching felt like. And what kind of teacher I wanted to be.

So when I set foot in Room 907, I didn't just return—I rose. Stronger. Wiser. And more ready than ever. Because sometimes, you have to lose a title to reclaim your truth.

And mine? Was always: *teacher.*

From August to December of 2024, something extraordinary happened. Without a title. Without an office. Without a nameplate on the door. Just me. A whiteboard. A plan. And a purpose. I led.

I led as a teacher, not from the front of the building, but from the heart of it. And what we accomplished? Numbers don't usually tell the whole story—but in this case, they shouted. Every teacher in my department saw measurable, meaningful gains. Not one. Not some. Every single one.

And in my own classroom? My students increased by 18 percentage points in proficiency.

Let that sink in: 18 percentage points in just a few months—at a Title I school where the odds are stacked, the resources are scarce, and the stories students carry are heavier than any backpack.

These are the kids who are often underestimated, overlooked, and under-supported. The kids who come to school hungry—not just for food, but for safety, for belonging, for someone who sees past the data points and into their potential.

At Bare Minimum Magnet Middle, progress like that wasn't just a win—it was a revolution. Because when you lead with purpose, you can shift a culture without a name tag. And when you lead from within, students rise. Teachers rise. The entire energy of a building rises.

That's what happened. We built something. Quietly. Boldly. Together. The Literacy Department—once written off, now writing a new story.

And me? I wasn't just teaching reading and writing. I was modeling resilience. Redefining what leadership could look like when it's driven not by titles, but by impact. Because sometimes, the most powerful changes don't start in an office. They start in a classroom. They start with a teacher who remembers that the most radical thing you can do in education… is believe.

Around the midpoint of the school year, an announcement stirred a quiet buzz across campus: one of the assistant principals was retiring. A coveted seat at the table was opening, and for the first time since my return to the classroom, I felt something rise in me that I hadn't dared name in a while—hope. Not just any hope. Empowered hope. Because of her.

Ms. Williams-DeVyne—the woman who greeted me with warmth, trusted my leadership, and let my work speak louder than my wounds—made me feel like I belonged again. Like I could reach for more without apology. So I applied. Not because I expected a guarantee, but because I knew I was ready to reclaim the part of me that had been shelved, bruised, and nearly silenced. I had fallen back in love with teaching—but I still believed in my capacity to lead. To rise. To rewrite the ending.

The interview came, and I showed up—not as someone trying to prove their worth, but as someone who knew it. I nailed it. I walked out feeling strong, aligned, and proud. But I didn't get the job.

And oddly enough… I didn't feel defeated. Because the very next day, my principal pulled me aside. She didn't sugarcoat it. She didn't sidestep it. She told me the truth.

"This wasn't just an interview," she said. *"It was an olive branch."*

She wanted to see firsthand what I was capable of. She already knew the rumors. She knew about the non-renewal, the gossip, the damage done by someone else's narrative. But she also knew something deeper—my truth. And this interview? It was her way of letting me reclaim it.

She wanted the district leadership team to see me in action. To hear the clarity in my voice, the strength behind my answers, the vision I had not just for classrooms, but for a campus. This was my moment—not to win a position, but to take back my narrative. And I did.

I didn't walk away with a title that day. But I walked away with something more valuable. Redemption. Visibility. A seat back at the table—not because it was handed to me, but because I pulled up a chair and reminded everyone exactly who I was. And sometimes? That's the real win.

There wasn't a single defining moment that told me I was where I needed to be. It was quieter than that. More subtle. But unmistakably real.

It was the way students lingered after class—not because they needed help with an assignment, but because they just wanted to talk. To exist. To be seen. It was the way a student who barely spoke in August was suddenly raising their hand in October. The way another one, who used to skip school regularly, started showing up every day, parked in their usual seat, waiting for the lesson to begin.

It was in the mornings, when I'd open my classroom door and find a handful of kids already waiting—backpacks slung over one shoulder, earbuds in, but eyes looking toward me like I had something they couldn't find anywhere else.

It was in the laughter. In the way we built a classroom culture where mistakes weren't punished—they were part of the process. Where we could talk about grammar and grief, Shakespeare and self-worth, sentence structure and survival—all in the same period. My classroom wasn't just a space for academics. It was a sanctuary. A soft place to land. A room where every kid, no matter their story, knew they mattered. And slowly, I started to matter to them too.

That was the affirmation. Not in applause, not in awards, not in any one grand gesture—but in the way they kept showing up. And how, without even knowing it, they helped me show up for myself again.

This wasn't just teaching. *This was healing.*

Chapter Nineteen

Eat, Pray, Puerto Rico

Grief has a strange way of traveling with you—even when you think you've packed light.

The trip to Puerto Rico wasn't planned. Not really. It started with a hug at my uncle's funeral. A reconnection. A cousin. A conversation. Maddie mentioned taking her son to the island for his 18th birthday, and before I could filter myself, I blurted out, *"I'm coming too."* There wasn't hesitation—just laughter, then love. *"You better,"* she said. And just like that, I was in.

Perla flew out with me for the weekend, the kind of friend who doesn't need much convincing to hop on a plane when healing calls. And healing was calling—loudly. It had been nearly a year since the day my career collapsed in slow motion, orchestrated by the hands of someone who should've been my leader. I'd spent twelve months rebuilding what she tried to ruin. Not just my résumé, but my spirit. My peace. My sense of purpose.

I stayed in my godmother Joie's home—warm and worn in the way only homes with history can be. On the first evening, as the sun bowed down behind the hills and washed the backyard in a golden haze, I stepped outside barefoot and felt the kind of stillness you don't find on the mainland. And that's when I felt her…my mother.

She was there in the breeze, in the glow, in the sudden ache behind my eyes. Tears welled—not from pain, but from the overwhelming beauty of survival. I stood there, free and full of gratitude. Gratitude that I had survived the year that tried to break me. That I had found joy again in the wreckage. That I had become someone she'd be proud of.

For the first time in what felt like forever, my tears weren't about loss. They were about becoming.

This wasn't just a trip. It was a return. Not just to the island—but to myself.

And now, I sit here—on Joie's back patio, surrounded by coquí lullabies and the scent of sea salt and plantains still lingering in the air—trying to put words to a feeling I can barely hold. My laptop open, a breeze dancing across the keyboard like it knows what I'm about to say before I do.

I am writing this here. In the middle of it. Not from a distance or in hindsight, but from the very heart of my becoming.

I came here thinking I needed a break. What I found was a mirror.

Puerto Rico has this way of showing you who you are without saying a word. The mountains don't care about your résumé. The waves don't ask who hurt you. And the sun doesn't ask for permission to touch every part of you—even the parts you've hidden. And somehow, in that kind of silence, I found clarity louder than anything I've heard in months.

I think we often tell ourselves that growth is this loud, roaring thing. That it looks like declarations and job titles and applause. But what if growth is quiet? What if it's this—me, barefoot in a borrowed chair, hearing the hum of the island while realizing I'm no longer angry?

Not at her.

Not at the system.

Not at myself.

Because while a title was stripped away from me in an office where my truth wasn't welcome, here—under this sky, with no agenda, no obligation—I found something else: the permission to expand.

I am not the same man who boarded that plane on my way here.

Back then, I was still trying to prove something. Still performing grief and resilience like it was a job interview. Still hoping someone would see me and say, *"You're good enough. We made a mistake."*

But here? The only approval I need is my own. The only voice that matters is the one inside me saying: *You did it. You made it. You're still standing.*

Maybe that's the thing about places that feel like home. They don't fix you. They just remind you that you were never broken to begin with—just bruised, just tired, just waiting for the right soil to grow again.

And let me tell you, this soil? It's fertile with forgiveness. With softness. With hope.

With Perla by my side, San Juan never stood a chance.

She brought the spark, the city brought the rhythm, and together we turned the weekend into a memory. We danced through the night with glitter in our smiles and rum in our systems, shedding stress like sweat beneath the neon lights. For a few hours, we weren't educators or worriers or warriors—we were just two best friends, twinning in joy, our laughter loud enough to make the past jealous.

Then came Jobos Beach.

An afternoon wrapped in sunshine, seafoam, and the kind of happiness that doesn't need translation. With sand between our toes and the waves applauding us from a distance, I looked around—at Perla, at Maddie and her son, at his two friends—and realized how rare it is to feel so held by both place and people at the same time. No expectations. No performance. Just presence.

Maddie and I talked into the wee hours of the night, our conversations peeling back years of distance. We spoke about grief, our parents, relationships, life, and the ways it surprises us—sometimes painfully, sometimes beautifully. She saw parts of me that most people skip over. The parts still healing. The parts that, on this island, didn't feel so heavy anymore.

And then there was Ethan, her son.

Eighteen and teetering on the edge of adulthood, he reminded me so much of myself. Not just because we're both gay, but because I could see that quiet flicker in him—the one that says *I'm figuring this out in real-time, but I'm going to be okay.* He doesn't know it yet, but the world is about to try and put him in a box—hand him a label and expect him to wear it like a uniform. I just hope he remembers he was born to break the mold, not fit into it.

We shared glances, jokes, and passing wisdom between moments, and though I didn't lecture or linger, I made sure he knew I saw him. Because sometimes, being seen is the very thing that helps you survive.

And then there were the quiet hours—the ones where I was completely alone. No noise, no scrolling, no to-do lists. Just me, my laptop, and the island. I read. I wrote. I rested. I walked barefoot on the beach and let the wind flirt with my hair. I didn't need a therapist or a breakthrough—I just needed a little peace. A place to breathe.

Puerto Rico gave me that. It gave me back to me.

Perla flew back home on Monday—you know, to her husband and kids and all that domestic goddess realness. I was a little sad to see her go, not just because she's my partner-in-chaos, but because this was our first official "friendcation." Sun, sass, and shared sunscreen. It meant something.

Even though the house felt a little quieter without her energy bouncing off the walls, I wasn't mad—mostly because I still had six more days of island time to soak in. Healing isn't on a schedule, and apparently, neither was I.

In typical Chris Machado fashion... I found someone. On Grindr, no less.

He was Dominican and Puerto Rican—just like me. A year

younger, slightly taller, with a killer smile and eyes so deep I swear I could see his spirit wading in them. I logged on looking for a little flirtation, maybe even some fleeting fun, but he was searching for something more: connection, conversation, and a little chemistry.

And to my surprise, he had me curious. He was warm, grounded, and refreshingly real. His messages weren't laced with tired one-liners or surface-level small talk—he asked questions, he listened, he engaged. So when he offered to pick me up and take me to this cozy, authentic Puerto Rican restaurant tucked away from the tourist traps, I said yes. And I'm glad that I did.

As we sat across from each other, I realized we shared more than just roots. We shared rhythm. Laughter. Similar stories told from different coasts. We talked about family, about identity, about how hard it can be to feel at home in two places at once. It felt... easy.

But if there's one thing I know about myself, it's this: I crave connection, but I'm not built for long-distance fairy tales. I've tried them before. The late-night calls. The countdowns to the next visit. The ache of absence. They can be beautiful, but eventually, the time zones wear you down.

And this? This was a vacation. A chapter. A moment. Or so I thought. Because sometimes, the person you think will be your anchor turns out to be just a wave—and the real story is still waiting, just beyond the shore.

Still, when the night was supposed to end, I found myself wanting just a little more time.

We'd planned to hit up a billiards bar and play a few rounds of pool, but the place was closed—so I pivoted. I invited him back to the Airbnb.

Now, most people would pause at the idea of bringing a Grindr date to a family gathering, but I'm not most people. And Maddie? She's not most cousins. He walked in and charmed everyone instantly. Even the teens were vibing. Before we knew it, we were all sitting around the table, locked in a heated game of dominoes that stretched until 2:30 in the morning.

There was no script. No pressure. Just laughter, a few competitive slams on the table, and a night that somehow made the island feel even more like home.

That was the first—and last—time I saw him.

A few days later, he texted me, saying he didn't feel up for meeting again because he sensed his energy wasn't being fully reciprocated—and honestly, he wasn't wrong. Sure, he was a stand-up, stable guy, the kind anyone would be lucky to meet. But the truth? The spark just wasn't there for me.

Those next few days slipped by like a warm breeze—we spent them stretched out on the sand, sipping piña coladas that tasted like sunshine, and feasting on crispy pastelillos (empanadas), golden alcapurrias, and perfectly salty bacalaitos until our bellies were full and our hearts even fuller. We couldn't resist going back to Crash Boat Beach—not once, but twice.

Crash Boat Beach, cradled along the northwestern coast of Aguadilla, is more than just a postcard-perfect stretch of Puerto Rico—it's a feeling. Once a rescue boat dock, its faded pier now serves a different mission: launching joyful souls into the clear, blue Caribbean.

With each leap off the weathered concrete and splash into the sea, you don't just cool off—you let go. It's sun-soaked and full of life, a place where time lingers, laughter carries on the breeze, and the memories cling to you like salt on your skin.

Somewhere in between the late-night dominoes, the coquí lullabies, and the ocean kisses at Jobos and Crash Boat Beach, I realized something.

This trip wasn't an escape. It was a return. A reclamation. A quiet rebellion against everything that once tried to convince me I had to be "on" all the time. On point. On edge. On the verge of proving my worth.

But here—on this island that knew my bloodline before I did—I wasn't performing.

I was being.

I didn't come to Puerto Rico to fix myself. I came to remember who I was before I started shrinking to survive. And the island? She held up a mirror so tenderly, so truthfully, that I couldn't look away. She didn't just show me who I am. She reminded me of who I've always been.

I've always been the boy who knew how to survive. The one who sat with grief when it was too big for his little hands but held it anyway. The one who learned to make people laugh even when his heart was heavy. The one who carried his family's dreams on his back, even when the weight bent him in half.

I've always been the man who refused to stay small. Who fought for his students, for his friends, for the version of himself that the world kept trying to silence. I've been the one who lost and loved and risked again, who sat in the quiet after the chaos and asked himself: *What now?* —and then stood back up.

I've been the one who broke, yes—but I've also been the one who rebuilt. Over and over. Fiercely. Tenderly. Without losing the parts of me that matter most: my softness, my fire, my stubborn belief that I was made for more.

That's who I've always been.

Grief may have followed me here, but it didn't lead the way. It sat in the backseat, quiet, respectful—even a little surprised by how much joy I'd found along the ride.

I've always been good at surviving. At reinventing myself after heartbreak, after loss, after the kind of endings no one prepares you for. But Puerto Rico reminded me that reinvention doesn't always have to be reactive. Sometimes it's just a soft returning. A remembering. A whisper that says: *you're allowed to take up space*—not just in rooms, but in your own story.

And maybe, just maybe… healing isn't always about moving on. Sometimes, it's about coming home.

To anyone reading this who's been waiting for the right

moment—to take the trip, to say yes, to start over, to let go. This is your sign: go anyway. Book the flight. Say yes to the plan that scares you a little. Take the vacation you swear you don't have the time or money for. Because I promise you, experience will always be worth more than the dollars in your account.

The world can take titles. It can take jobs. It can even take people you love. But it cannot take the memories you create when you finally choose you.

Puerto Rico didn't fix me.

It freed me.

And the version of myself I'm walking away with? He's not just healed. He's whole. Not because life's been easy. Not because the pain magically disappeared. But because I did the work. I stood in the rubble of what they tried to destroy—and decided to rebuild anyway. Slower. Stronger. Brick by brick. With boundaries. With belief. With becoming.

Because wholeness isn't about perfection. It's about *integration*. About taking every scar, every stumble, every second-guess—and stitching it into something sacred. Something that says: *I survived that... and I'm still soft.*

The man I am today isn't just a product of pain. He is the proof of perseverance. The result of prayer. The reward of choosing myself—again and again—even when the world told me I wasn't worth the risk.

Puerto Rico was never the destination. It was the exhale. The earned pause. The reminder that after everything—after the demotion, the breakdowns, the heartbreak, the grief—I'm still here. I'm still standing.

No title. No apology. No permission needed. This trip didn't change me. It celebrated me.

And as I sit here, wrapping up this chapter on a borrowed patio in the middle of the Caribbean, I realize this isn't the end of my story. It's the part where I finally start writing it—on my own terms.

Chapter Twenty

Anchored, Humbled, and Whole Again

My last day in Puerto Rico was a perfect blend of island magic and the kind of cinematic romance you only see in dreamy rom-coms. Maddie and I spent the afternoon at Jobos Beach, surrounded by pure Puerto Rican joy—families gathered around full-course beachside meals, men slamming dominoes on wooden tables, and Bad Bunny's voice spilling from nearly every speaker, soundtracking the sunlit chaos.

And, because apparently I'm a glutton for punishment with a flair for masochism, I had connected with someone else on Grindr.

He was supposed to meet me at the beach—just a casual hangout—but when the truth surfaced, he admitted his car was recently totaled and was stuck borrowing his mom's car to run errands. He hadn't told me sooner because he was embarrassed. Honestly, I could've—maybe *should've*—let the conversation end there, but destiny had other plans for my final night on the island. So I offered to pick him up so we could still grab dinner.

Half-nervous and half-obsessed with finding the perfect outfit, I took too long getting ready. Even though he only lived seven minutes away, by the time I arrived, the restaurant he had planned for us was closed—and I felt like an absolute ass. But the moment he stepped outside to greet me, all that embarrassment melted away.

He carried the effortless beauty of his Puerto Rican roots—pale, almost porcelain skin that shimmered softly against the thick, inky waves of his black hair, giving him an ethereal, striking presence—delicate at first glance, but quietly captivating beneath the surface. His deep, soulful eyes didn't just meet yours—they held you, soft and magnetic in a way that asked nothing and offered everything.

But it was his lips that stole the moment—full, perfectly shaped, the kind of lips made for slow, lingering kisses and whispered promises under the stars. There was a quiet allure in the way he moved, a subtle confidence wrapped in gentleness, like he was a love letter penned in the curve of his smile and the warmth of his gaze.

And standing there, looking at him for the first time in person, I felt it—that irresistible pull, as if the universe had hit pause just so I could commit this moment to memory, etching the way he looked into a part of me that would refuse to let it fade.

With the restaurant closed, he pivoted without missing a beat and took me to Pirate Canteen, a mojito bar tucked away in Alta Mar, Aguadilla—known for serving the best mojitos in all of Puerto Rico. From there, we wandered into a quieter kind of magic.

Afterward, he took me to La Casa del Árbol Más Grande de Puerto Rico in Parque Colón—the home of the largest tree on the island, a massive, centuries-old ceiba tree said to be a living monument of strength and endurance.

And beneath that towering giant, under the vast Puerto Rican sky, we shared our first kiss. It was soft. Slow. Electric. The kind of kiss that makes you question every long-held belief you've had about long-distance love. The kind that doesn't ask for logic—only presence.

We ended the night walking along Paseo Tablado de Isabela, a winding wooden boardwalk that stretches for nearly a mile, the waves whispering beside us as the stars seemed to cheer us on. His laugh echoed beneath the moonlight; a sound that felt instantly familiar. Our conversation flowed like a current—fluid, effortless, alive. There was quick wit, thoughtful insight, and something deeper pulsing beneath his every word. Something sincere.

Eventually, I brought him back to my place, where the night blurred into something timeless.

Something neither of us wanted to end—but as always, reality caught up, and the only thing that finally pulled us apart was the fact that he had to get to work.

Before I left, I felt this undeniable urge to leave him something—a relic, a memory of me and our night together. I settled on my anchor necklace, the one I had worn while we were together.

My flight was scheduled to leave before he'd even get off work, but Maddie was staying a few extra days, so I handed it to her along with a note I wrote for him so that he could pick it up on his way home:

I'm so glad I met you — even if it was on my very last night in Puerto Rico—because now you've given me an even better reason to come back sooner.

Your smile, your laugh, and the connection we shared last night have stayed with me, and honestly, I just can't let it go.

I wanted to leave you with something meaningful, a piece of me that captures what this trip has meant to me: my anchor necklace.

This journey anchored me in ways I never expected, and now, you'll be my anchor to Puerto Rico—until I return.

I can't wait to see you again. Until next time, my love.

Too much? Too soon? Maybe for someone else. But not for me. This is who I am, and I refuse to dim my light just to make someone else feel comfortable sitting in the dark. I won't let past heartbreaks or failed connections jade me into holding back. I love fully, or I don't love at all.

Before I took off, I sent him a quick message letting him know I'd left a little something at the house for him to pick up after work.

I also gave Maddie one mission: *"Get the tea for me…and let me know your read on him."*

And boy, did she deliver.

She told me he was sweet—but not just in the performative way. The *real* kind. The kind that shows up in the little things: The way he spoke respectfully. The quiet confidence in how he carried himself. The way his face lit up when he talked about his family.

Maddie said he was raised right—with values you can't fake. There was a warmth to him that told her everything she needed to know. He wasn't arrogant or over-polished. He was grounded. Genuine. Sure of himself in a way that doesn't ask for attention—just earns it.

And the part that nearly undid me? He told her he was already thinking about when he could come visit me in Florida.

When I landed, I opened a message from him. He said my note brought tears to his eyes. That he was going to wear the necklace to keep a piece of me close until we could meet again. That his world had *exploded*—in the best possible way—the moment I kissed him. And that he'd never felt a connection as undeniable as what he felt with me.

Mission: *Accomplished.*

And now? We still talk every day. Messages that bridge the distance, reminders of a night that feels like it shouldn't have just been a moment but a beginning. We're both already looking forward to the next time we see each other—and maybe, just maybe, this is the universe telling me that sometimes the most unexpected encounters are the ones that leave the deepest imprint on your heart.

For someone who's always been skeptical about long-distance relationships, he made me pause and reconsider. Maybe it wasn't about the miles or the logistics—maybe it was about the pull, the wanting, the undeniable sense that this was something worth holding onto. And for the first time in a long time, I found myself wondering if some connections are strong enough to rewrite the rules I thought I knew.

Where does this part of my story end? Stay tuned—because some flames don't burn out; they linger softly, waiting to ignite the next chapter when you least expect it. Maybe the most beautiful stories are the ones still unfolding, just beyond the horizon.

Waking up back at home for work after ten days in the slice of heaven that is Puerto Rico was brutal. I snoozed my alarm for nearly an hour before finally launching myself out of bed, jolted by the reminder that we had a faculty meeting first thing that morning.

As we gathered in the media center, our principal, Ms. Williams-Devyne, stood before us with an announcement: she was being transferred to another school next year.

But then came the silver lining: all early indicators from our most recent data pointed to something we hadn't seen in a *decade*—after years of being stuck at a C, our school was finally on track to become a B school, and I felt like I'd been knocked unconscious and brought back to life in the same breath.

Why? Because Ms. Williams-Devyne had taken a chance on me when others wouldn't. She led not just with strategy, but with *heart*—and in that single year together, we had achieved something remarkable. She reminded me that leadership rooted in compassion isn't weakness; it's the secret weapon.

And then, it hit me even harder—as the kids started pouring into my classroom, it wasn't just the usual chatter or routine welcome. They were *beaming*, running up to me with hugs, peppering me with questions about my trip, and telling me how much they had missed me. That moment cracked me open in the best possible way.

Because after the kind of year I'd had—clawing my way back from personal and professional setbacks, questioning my worth, wondering if I still had it in me—to be met with that pure, unfiltered joy from my students was everything. It was a reminder that despite the storms I'd weathered, I was still standing, still making an impact, and still exactly where I was meant to be.

Not because life finally played fair. Not because I got everything I prayed for. But because I kept going when it didn't. Because I rebuilt when I was shattered. Because I showed up for myself, even when it felt like no one else would.

This trip—this chapter—wasn't about escaping. It was about remembering. Remembering who I've always been beneath the titles, the trauma, and the timelines I thought I had to meet. I'm a lover. A teacher. A writer. A survivor. And maybe most of all—I'm someone who refuses to let the dark define the ending.

Puerto Rico gave me back my breath. My students reminded me why I fight. And he—*my Prince*—showed me that love doesn't have to be loud to be life-changing. Sometimes, it's just a quiet "be safe" at the end of the night, a kiss under a ceiba tree, or a note wrapped in vulnerability and left behind like a breadcrumb for fate to follow.

I don't know what comes next—not in love, not in life. But for the first time in a long time, I'm not afraid of the unknown. I'm excited by it. Because the boy who once begged the universe to throw him a lifeline has become the man who built one.

I'm whole. I'm healed. But even healed people have soft spots.

Perla once told me something that landed right in the deepest part of me:

"You are inherently worthy, even in your quietest, messiest, most uncertain moments. You don't need to overperform or overexplain to be valuable. But sometimes, it seems like you forget that. You carry this deep wisdom and emotional intelligence, yet you often operate like you still have to 'prove' yourself—to be more, do more, give

more—when just being is more than enough. I see a pattern of self-sabotage not because you're broken, but because some part of you hasn't fully accepted how whole you already are. You carry light and depth that others feel instinctively—even when you can't quite see it in the mirror."

And Joie echoed the same sentiment, just in her own grounded way: *"You can't hold onto your grief and trauma. Healing means fully accepting the joy, the laughter, and the love you deserve."*

Being back on the island this time wasn't just a reset—it was a reckoning. Joie, as always, had this way of mothering me without smothering me. Of making me feel safe while still holding up a mirror. She never pushes, never lectures. She simply creates space—for honesty, for softness, for truth. In the kitchen over arroz con gandules. In the car as we sang along to old Salsa songs. In the kitchen with a glass of wine and the moonlight whispering between us.

She reminded me—gently but firmly—that I cannot keep holding hands with my grief and expect joy to find its way in. That healing isn't about revisiting my pain on a loop, but about letting it take its rightful place in my story... not the leading role.

She and Perla helped me see that just because I've learned how to survive doesn't mean I've fully allowed myself to thrive. And that thriving requires more than resilience. It requires acceptance. It requires joy. And most of all—it requires me to believe I deserve it.

They reminded me that I don't need to perform my worth. I don't need to win love by being everything to everyone. I just need to be. Because the right people won't love me despite my depth. They'll love me because of it.

And even though I've done so much healing—even though I know I'm whole—I still find myself wondering if I'm asking for too much when all I really want is to be chosen.

That's the part I'm still working through.

So here I am. Still soft. Still strong.

Still learning how to receive the love I've spent my whole life trying to give away. And maybe, just maybe, learning to love myself enough to stop settling for pieces.

Chapter Twenty One

A Life Rewritten

This summer, silence became its own kind of rejection. I had applied for the assistant principal position—the one I wanted so badly it felt like a lifeline. I checked my email every morning, every afternoon, every night, hoping for a subject line with my name on it, waiting for the phone to light up with a call that never came. No interview. No second chance. Just silence.

The universe, it seemed, had answered me with a *no*.

And as if that wasn't enough, life kept coming. Evelyn's cancer had returned, pulling her back into the exhausting rhythm of chemo treatments. Just weeks after the family reunion—the first time in decades we had gathered so fully, so joyfully—another uncle passed away. Loss didn't even knock on the door anymore; it just walked in, uninvited, and sat down at the table like it lived here.

I wish I could say I rose to the challenge. That I pulled myself up, dusted myself off, and faced it all with the kind of strength people like to post about online. But the truth? Instead of climbing out of the hole, I let it swallow me. I curled up inside it, wrapping myself in a blanket of self-pity, letting the weight of disappointment and grief crush me from the inside out.

And here's the thing: I've studied grief. I've lived through trauma.

I've written about healing. But I still forget, sometimes, that spiraling isn't healing. That replaying the pain doesn't rewrite the story.

The problem, and maybe the gift, is that I'm not built like most people. My heart has no dimmer switch. I feel everything, deeply, almost violently. Other people's pain doesn't just touch me; it lives inside me. I carry it like it's stitched into my skin, a tapestry of scars and tenderness. And in moments like these, that weight feels unbearable.

But as the summer ended and a new school year began, life gave me another unexpected kind of lifeline.

I walked back into the classroom—back to bulletin boards and the hum of fluorescent lights, to the awkward, nervous laughter of kids still figuring out who they are. Only this time, things looked different. For the first time in my career, I was assigned all advanced classes, grades seven and eight.

My students came to me carrying something extraordinary: a 97% overall passing rate on their end-of-year state assessment.

Ninety-seven percent.

To some, that might sound like just another number. To me, it meant *everything*.

Because for over a decade, I had taught the students who struggled the most—the ones the system labeled "at-risk," the ones who had been written off before they even walked through the door. I had been their advocate, their cheerleader, their sometimes last line of defense against giving up. And I loved them fiercely. But it was exhausting, often thankless work that left me questioning whether I was making a dent in the cycles of failure the world had built around them.

Now, I stood in front of a different group of kids—the so-called "smartest" in the school. Kids whose challenges weren't about catching up but about being pushed further. And here's what I realized: this, too, was a calling. Their brilliance wasn't an accident, but it wasn't a guarantee either. They still needed a teacher who believed in them. They still needed someone to remind them that excellence isn't just measured by test scores, but by how they carry that excellence into the world.

On my very first day, during my introductory PowerPoint, I gave them a glimpse into who I am. My story. My scars. My journey. And without even realizing it, I handed them my recipe for success:

- Believe in yourself—even when doubt feels louder than confidence.

- Choose to surround yourself with people who lift you higher and remind you of your worth.

- Work relentlessly for your dreams, especially on the days when the tunnel feels endless and the light seems far away.

I realized, as I spoke those words, that I wasn't just teaching them—I was reminding myself. In their faces, I saw pieces of my own story staring back at me.

It felt, in many ways, like a mirror to my own life. For years, I've been climbing uphill, carrying weight that threatened to crush me, wondering if I'd ever see the summit. And suddenly, here I was—leading rooms full of students who represented the very best of what education could be.

Their success reminded me of my own resilience. Their hunger for more reminded me that I, too, was still reaching.

When I started this book, I thought it would end differently. I imagined myself at the seat of the metaphorical table of a school leader, title on the door, keys on the lanyard, proof that I had finally "arrived." But life has shown me something deeper: my power has never come from a title, a salary, or an office. My power is in how I carry my story, how I show up for others, and how I continue to rise—again and again.

Perla, as she often does, reminded me of what I sometimes forget: that I carry a grounded, unwavering belief that life will ultimately guide me where I'm meant to be—even if the path is unclear or rocky in the moment. It's not blind optimism. It's a kind of spiritual confidence, a reminder that the universe doesn't punish—it *redirects*.

And so, I choose to believe that things don't fall apart to hurt us. They fall apart to realign us. To refine us. To return us.

And right now—even without the title, even without the desk at the head of the table—I know this: *I am exactly where I'm supposed to be.*

Because maybe this was never about the title. Maybe it was about every moment that brought me here—the heartbreaks that cracked me open, the friendships that stitched me back together, the classrooms that reminded me of my purpose, the family who proved that love survives distance, death, and time.

It was about my mother, Maria, whose hands taught me that food was love and sacrifice was strength. It was about my father, Angel, who showed me resilience even when his own demons tried to take him down. It was about my brother, whose struggles mirrored the kids I would one day teach, reminding me that no child is disposable.

It was about Julia, whose unwavering support reminds me that being a pillar for others can be its own kind of courage. About Antonio, whose quiet steadiness shows that true strength often speaks in actions, not words.

About Evelyn, who has taught me more about faith in the face of sickness than I could ever learn from any sermon.

About Madeline and Roberto, who have stood beside me in both struggle and triumph, including as we hosted our first family reunion this summer—70 people gathered under one roof, laughter and music echoing through the walls, proof that even fractured families can find their way back to one another.

About my aunts, uncles and cousins, the Frias and Machado bloodlines, whose stories run through my veins, whose losses still shape my prayers.

It was about standing in Times Square with Miles, learning that love doesn't always last but it always leaves a mark.

About Lyric, and how a ring and a shared home can't hold together what honesty can't sustain.

About Jordan and the others—chapters of my heart that each

taught me something about who I was, and who I refuse to be. About Puerto Rico—not just an island, but my very own sanctuary—where the ocean baptized me in second chances and reminded me that home is not always a place, but a feeling.

It was about Milo, my four-legged shadow, who anchored me through storms I didn't think I could survive.

About Perla, my sister by choice, who has never let me forget that I was born with a light inside me, even when others tried to dim it.

About friends like Cassie, Brenna, Kamille, and my warrior women—my chosen family—who reminded me, time and time again, that I am loved, even when I don't feel lovable.

And it was about my students—always, my students. The ones who walked into my classroom labeled "at-risk" and taught me that resilience is contagious. The ones now, with their 97% passing rate, who show me that brilliance isn't the absence of struggle but the refusal to stop striving.

And maybe that's why I see so much of myself in them. Their victories are reminders that the labels we carry don't define us—our choices do. Just as they've rewritten the narratives handed to them, I've had to rewrite my own. Because survival is not my story. Standing is not my story. My story is how I've learned to turn endings into beginnings, heartbreak into healing, and detours into destinations.

Grief taught me how fragile life can be, but love taught me how unshakable it really is. And when I look back now, I see that every loss, every failure, every tear was really just life making room—for new joy, new hope, new beginnings. The pieces I thought were shattered forever were never wasted. They became the mosaic of the person I was always meant to be.

This memoir began with loss.

It ends with love.

And between those two, a life has been rewritten.

Still, I stand.

And still, *I'm becoming.*

Epilogue
Dearest Reader, Still I Stand

If you've made it this far, then you've walked with me through it all—from the backseat of a rusted Nissan Sentra to the front lines of a Title I classroom. You've stood in the shadow of grief, sat with heartbreak, broken down in principals' offices, and healed—inch by inch, story by story.

I also imagine a few things are true:

You've laughed.

You've cried.

You've probably highlighted some line and whispered *"same."*

And maybe—just maybe—you've seen a bit of yourself in these pages. That was the point.

Because this book was never just about me. It was about us. Every misstep, every meltdown, every miracle—it's all stitched together with something we all know intimately: the ache of becoming. The longing for more. The sting of rejection. The roar of resilience. The beauty of beginning again, and again, and again.

When I first started on this journey, I was writing like I was racing—eager to get it all down, as if finishing the sentence could finally close the wound. One night, as I reread a particularly raw chapter, Perla called me. *"Stop,"* she said, her voice steady. *"You need to pause. You're not just writing this—you're reliving it. Don't sprint through your own pain. Sit with it. Feel it. Let it teach you something."*

She was right. I was so focused on documenting the past, I wasn't digesting it. And in doing so, I nearly skipped the part where the healing happens.

So I took a breath. Then another.

And I let the words become more than a manuscript. I let them become medicine. Because I'm still healing. And that's okay.

If life has taught me anything, it's this: healing doesn't come in a straight line. It's not a staircase—it's a damn dance floor. Two steps forward, three shots of tequila, one bad decision, and a dramatic spin back into therapy.

But even with the bruises and bad karaoke, we keep dancing. And somewhere in between the mess and the magic, we find our way.

This epilogue? It's not just a conclusion.

Because this is the part of the story where I don't just look back—I look forward. I don't know what comes next. I'm open, but let's dream big. Maybe it'll be a TED Talk. Or a limited series on HBO Max— Billy Porter narrating my inner monologue like its gospel with glitter, Matt Bomer playing me with just the right balance of heartbreak and perfect hair flips. Or maybe—just maybe—it'll be another classroom, another kid, another chance to remind someone that they're not invisible. That they matter.

But more than likely? It'll be a podcast. Hosted by me and Perla—because obviously. One episode per chapter. Raw, unfiltered, full of laughter, tears, and truth—complete with guest appearances from some of the unforgettable characters in these pages. The ones who shaped me, tested me, saved me. The ones who proved that chosen family is just as sacred as the one you're born into.

And if you've ever felt that kind of love—steady, earned, and electrifying—you'll know this next feeling well.

There's this moment—right before a curtain rises, right before a speaker steps up to the mic, right before a rollercoaster drops—where time stretches just a little. Where breath catches in your chest and your heart whispers, *this is it.*

That's where I'm standing now.

The end of this story. The beginning of another.

And maybe that's the thing about survival. About healing. About growth. We always imagine it as a destination—some glowing peak where the trauma disappears, the soundtrack swells, and everything finally makes sense. But the truth? Healing also isn't linear. It's circular. Messy. Repetitive. It's a dance between who you were, who you are, and who you're still becoming.

I never imagined I'd find myself here—finishing a memoir.

When I was younger, I thought by this age I'd have a doctorate, be a high school principal, married with kids. And while I don't have any of that... yet, I've learned something far more valuable: age doesn't define success. There's no timeline for dreams. No expiration date on becoming.

Trust the timing of your life—your pace is perfect for your path. This book you're holding is proof of that. To me, it means more than any of those milestones combined. Because so much of this story was written for the students I taught, the friends who stayed, the family who shaped me—and the parents who never got to finish writing their own legacies.

This is for them.

And this, somehow, is for me too.

Because for so long, I lived my life trying to be what everyone else needed—dependable, strong, put-together, surviving no matter the cost. I gave my energy to healing others, to showing up, to proving I was worth loving. But this book? This was the first time I showed up for myself.

Page after page, I told the truth—not just for the sake of storytelling, but to finally let me be seen. Not the version I filtered for approval. Not the polished image I performed to feel safe. But the real, cracked, healing, rising version—the one who dared to remember, to feel, and to speak.

So yes, this book is a tribute. A love letter. A legacy.

But it's also a reclamation.

It's the moment I stopped running from my story… and started owning it.

I've survived more versions of myself than I can count. The little boy clinging to the hem of his mom's dress. The teenager rehearsing how to say I'm gay out loud. The teacher who thought a title would fix the ache. The administrator who finally got his shot—only to lose it. The man who broke. The man who healed. The man who stood back up and said, *let's try again.*

And through all of it—all of it—there's been one unshakable truth: I'm still here. Still standing. Still fighting. Still writing.

I was raised by a mother who taught me that love was a verb, not a noun. Who faced HIV and a world that misunderstood her with more grace than most people manage in a lifetime. A woman who died far too young but left fingerprints on my soul that no amount of grief could erase. And a father who, while not perfect, passed down strength in ways I didn't fully understand until I needed it most.

I grew up in a house that didn't always feel like home. I came out in a world that didn't always feel safe. I lost people I loved. I chased love like it was oxygen and sometimes settled for the emotional equivalent of a firework—loud, fleeting, and more smoke than spark.

But I also found my tribe.

My chosen family. My warrior women. The brunch crew. The best friends I "collect" like limited edition Barbies. (Yes, I know how it sounds. No, I'm not changing. If you're my best friend reading this— relax. You're absolutely the favorite. Just… maybe don't ask where you rank on days that end in Y.)

They were there when I fell apart.

And when I tried to pretend I was fine. And when I stood in front of classrooms or stared down rejection letters or held the shaking pieces of myself in both hands, unsure of how to start again.

They were there. Still are.

And so were my students—the kids who walked into my classroom thinking they had nothing to offer and walked out knowing they were more than enough. The ones who reminded me why I started this journey in the first place. The ones who, in their own quiet, chaotic, miraculous way... saved me.

To my former students—this is for you, too.

I see you.

I am proud of you.

A huge part of who I've become—as a teacher, as a leader, as a person—has been shaped by the privilege of watching you grow. I've spent my career trying to be the educator I needed when I was your age. Someone who listened. Someone who believed in you even when you didn't believe in yourself yet. And if I did my job right, you walked away not just knowing how to analyze a poem—but knowing that your story mattered.

Now here you are: grown adults, out in the world, becoming everything I always hoped for you. Teachers. Nurses. Firefighters. Lawyers. Social Workers. Moms. Dads. One of you started a successful cleaning business. Another launched a personal training enterprise and released a book. One is an operations director for a car detailing company. One of you turned a school bus into a home. Epic. And a few of you—you know who you are—somehow turned likes and follows into full-blown careers as social media influencers. Truly iconic behavior.

You're out there building lives, healing others, breaking cycles, chasing dreams—and I couldn't be prouder.

Watching you become who you were always meant to be? It's been one of the greatest honors of my life.

If no one's told you lately—I'm still rooting for you. Always.

This book is called *Still I Stand* for a reason.

Because I've fallen. Hard.

I've failed. Loudly.

I'm not the same boy from New York who sat watching *Unsolved Mysteries* with a Häagen-Dazs chocolate bar and a head full of questions. I'm not the closeted teen staring at the boy with blue eyes across the Walgreens counter making my heart race. I'm not the broken twenty-something crying on the floor of my apartment, bottle in hand, wondering if I'll ever feel whole again.

I am every version of him. And I'm still becoming.

But now? I stand taller.

Because I've carried the weight of grief and still reached for joy.

Because I've loved and lost and still believe in love.

Because I've failed loudly, gotten back up silently, and dared to try again.

Because even when the world told me "no"—I rewrote the sentence.

Still I stand.

Not just as a teacher. Or a gay man. Or someone who's been underestimated in boardrooms and broken in bedrooms.

Still I stand—as proof.

Proof that you can survive the chapters you thought would end you. Proof that a second chance isn't a gift—it's a choice. Proof that you can rewrite your life even when the ink is smudged, and the pages are torn.

To my parents, who I lost too soon—I hope this makes you proud. I hope you see me, *really see me,* and know that your boy did not just survive.

He lived. He loved. He rose.

To my family—those bound by blood and those I chose along the way—you are the spine of this story. Your laughter, your prayers, your presence… your belief in me when I didn't believe in myself.

To my best friends—yes, all 74 of you—thank you for being the soundtrack to my healing. For turning up, holding space, and reminding me who the hell I am when I forget. You are my glitter-covered lifeboats in the storm.

Writing this book has been cathartic in ways I never knew I needed. Each chapter was a reckoning. A quiet confrontation with the ghosts I thought I'd already buried. Every sentence held a mirror to parts of me I had long ignored—some bruised, some brave, all begging to be seen.

Each revision wasn't just about crafting the perfect line. It was about letting go—of guilt, of shame, of the stories I told myself to survive. And as the pages began to stitch themselves together, so did I.

This hasn't just been a memoir.

It's been an exorcism of shame.

A reclamation of power.

A love letter to the boy who carried too much alone...

And the man who now knows he doesn't have to.

The ghost of Miles no longer haunts me. Writing about him felt like walking barefoot across the shards of a memory I once swore I'd buried—but instead of reopening old wounds, it helped me see the scar for what it really was: *healed*.

I don't need to keep bleeding to prove it mattered.

I don't need to sit in rooms I've already outgrown, hoping the furniture feels like home again. Miles isn't a villain—but he's not my ending either. He belongs to a version of me that was still trying to earn love by shrinking, pleasing, performing. And I've come too far to ever go back to that.

He found a version of forever—polished, predictable, tied with a bow. And in a moment when liquid courage spoke louder than he did, I heard it in his voice: sometimes, the safest path isn't the one that sets you free. But he took it anyway. And in doing so—he didn't choose me.

So now, I choose me. Not in spite of him, but in defiance of regret. In resistance to longing. In honor of the light I've fought like hell to reclaim. And somewhere between the heartbreak and healing…

I found something else. Someone else.

A person who doesn't make me question if I'm too much.

A person who makes "soft" feel like strength.

A person who shows up without needing to be chased.

He's a gentleman, in the way that feels rare these days.

Loyal to his core.

Respectful without performative gestures.

Handsome—like, walks-into-a-room-and-the-air-changes kind of handsome and makes my dormant butterflies remember how to fly.

And his kisses? They make my soul come alive—like a love letter traced across my lips, every word stitched in warmth and truth. A kind of poetry in a language I forgot I was fluent in, waking every part of me I thought had gone quiet.

Some might think it's a lot and call it intense. But after everything I've been through…I refuse to apologize for wanting something real.

So, if you're reading this, my Puerto Rican Prince—*yeah, you*—I hope these pages don't scare you off. I hope they draw you in. I hope you see me for exactly who I am—flaws, fire, and all. And I hope you choose to stay.

Because for the first time in a long time…

I'm not writing from heartbreak. I'm writing from hope.

And you? You might just be my next chapter.

For those wondering why I even included him in this memoir—yes, even without naming him—when we're still just getting to know each other... the answer is as simple as it is complicated.

I'm a hopeless romantic...

The kind who still believes in love letters, even if they're typed out in iMessage bubbles. The kind who overanalyzes song lyrics and assigns meaning to glances. I romanticize the hell out of late-night conversations, shared playlists, and the way someone says my name when they're half-asleep. I believe in sparks—not the kind that burn you, but the ones that light you up.

I'm the type who sees a good morning text as a love language and a shared dessert as a subtle promise. It's not about rushing toward a finish line. It's about how I show up. Open-hearted. Eyes wide. Willing to risk a bruise if there's even a chance at something real. And after everything I've been through, I'd rather keep loving like this—with foolish faith—than build a life padded with fear and 'what ifs.'

And every heartbreak, no matter how big or brief, teaches me something new—about people, about patterns, and about myself.

But here's what I won't do: I won't let those lessons harden me. I won't let disappointment build walls where I've worked so hard to plant windows and let the light in.

Because the truth is, I've done the work. I've held a mirror to my abandonment issues, thanks to years of therapy, some brutally honest self-reflection, and the insights of Dr. Amir Levine and Rachel Heller in *Attached. The New Science of Adult Attachment and How It Can Help You Find – and Keep – Love*. I'm no longer chasing unavailable love or mistaking anxiety for excitement.

I know now that I am worthy of the real thing—of love that isn't performative or punishing. Love that feels like exhaling. Love that stirs up butterflies that had long since gone still. Love that is thrilling, yes, but also grounding.

They say only fools rush in, right? Well then slap a crown on me and call me the King of Fools, because I rush in faster than a Florida storm rolls in around 2:00 p.m.

But in this season of revival, my Puerto Rican Prince reminded me of something I hadn't felt in a long time. He didn't complete me—because I was already whole—but he did reignite something beautiful: a belief that maybe, just maybe, love still had a little magic left for me.

I don't know what's waiting in the next chapter. But I'm turning the page with open arms. Because this time? I believe in the person I'm becoming.

While this book has been, in many ways, a letter—to my students, my friends, my family, and the version of me I've fought to become—it's also been a roadmap to forgiveness. Not just for the people who lifted me, but for those who hurt me, too.

Yes, even her…the principal from Chapter 16.

The one whose decisions altered the course of my career, and at the time, shattered my sense of worth.

For a long time, I carried that anger like armor—sharp, protective, necessary. But page by page, as I wrote through the rise and the fall, the laughter and the grief, something inside me softened. Not because I forgot. Not because the pain wasn't real. But because I finally understood that holding onto bitterness only tethers you to the past.

She doesn't get to own the narrative of my downfall anymore—because I reclaimed it. She doesn't sit at the final chapter.

I do.

And the truth is... I don't wish her harm. I wish her healing. I wish her clarity. I wish her the ability to lead with the kind of love I've learned to give myself.

Because as much as it hurt—and it did—her actions forced a reckoning I'd been putting off for far too long. In some twisted, backhanded way... this book might not exist without that unraveling.

Sometimes the person who knocks the wind out of you is also the one who pushes you toward your purpose. And while I may never get an apology, I've given her the one thing that let me move forward—my forgiveness.

Because forgiveness isn't about forgetting. It's about remembering without rage, and walking away without the weight.

And in this epilogue, where every thread finds its way home, I want to say this out loud: I forgive her.

Not for her sake—but for mine.

Because healing doesn't just happen in silence or solitude—it happens in community, in connection, in the moments where we choose to rebuild instead of retreat.

Which is why, this summer, I brought to life something my family had never done before—our first ever family reunion. For three unforgettable days at my uncle's house in New Jersey, we welcomed over 70 relatives under one roof, many reuniting after years apart, others meeting for the very first time. The weekend overflowed with love, laughter, and endless plates of food—pizza and wings on Friday night, rice, beans, plantains, and pulled pork on Saturday, and a full Dominican brunch that felt like a hug from our ancestors on Sunday.

For a family like ours—fractured by loss, stitched back together with time, grace, and effort—this reunion wasn't just a party. It was a homecoming. It was proof that no matter how far we've scattered, the roots still run deep, binding us in ways distance can't undo.

And maybe the timing wasn't accidental. Because this year... marks 30 years since I lost my mother. And now, I'm 36— around the same age she was when she took her last breath. There's something sacred and unsettling about that.

Like the universe brought me full circle to understand just how young she really was. I've been chasing her memory my whole life... and somehow, this year, I caught up.

Three decades since that little boy stood in front of her casket, not fully understanding that life as he knew it had just cracked open. And now, here I am—releasing the book she never got to read. The story she never got to see unfold. But I like to think she's been reading every word along the way.

I wrote this book to honor her, to speak the truth she never got to tell, and to live the life she never got to finish. And I can't think of a better way to commemorate her legacy than with the reunion of a family she helped build…and the voice of a son she never stopped loving.

I've come to realize that honoring someone's legacy isn't just about telling their story—it's about telling your own honestly, too. That means confronting not just the pain others caused you, but the ways you've sometimes gotten in your own way.

Because the truth is, healing isn't always about what's been done to you. Healing also means taking a look at the role you play in your own suffering. It's a tough truth to swallow—especially when life has already handed you more grief than most people unpack in a lifetime.

It's easy to point to the people who left, the systems that failed, the love that didn't stay, and say, "That's why I hurt." And yes—those moments mattered. They shaped me. Bruised me. Some nearly broke me.

But the hardest mirror to stand in front of? The one that reflects the choices I made while I was bleeding.

The times I stayed too long. Shrunk myself too small. Silenced my needs in the name of love. The relationships I poured into like they were fountains when they were actually wells run dry. The jobs I clung to for validation, when deep down I already knew they were draining my soul. The apologies I gave out like candy while I was starving for someone to just understand me.

For a long time, I thought healing meant rewriting what had been done to me. But I've learned that true healing means owning what I've done to myself—with compassion, not shame. It means sitting with the version of me who was just trying to survive, and saying, *"You did the best you could. But we don't have to do it like that anymore."*

That's what this journey has been. A slow, painful, liberating process of unlearning. Of calling myself in—not out. Of forgiving others, yes—but also forgiving the younger me who didn't yet know how to protect his own peace. And now? I'm no longer asking for permission to be whole. I'm choosing it—day by day, decision by decision.

Because healing doesn't always look like light pouring in. Sometimes, it looks like a quiet confrontation with yourself. And the courage to finally say: *"I deserve better. Let's start now."*

Finally, to you, dearest reader… (Yes, that is a *Bridgerton* reference—because sometimes, healing looks less like therapy and more like Lady Whistledown spilling the tea.)

Here's what I'll leave you with:

After all the pain, the plot twists, the healing, the heartbreaks, the quiet victories, and the loud rebirths… this is what remains. Healing isn't always boisterous. Sometimes, it's just seeing yourself clearly in the mirror for the first time.

Clarity is power.

Vulnerability is strength.

And never—ever—dim your light just to make someone else feel more comfortable in the dark.

If something—or someone—makes your soul come alive, don't second-guess it.

Don't dilute your joy to fit into spaces that were never built to hold your brilliance.

Don't play it cool when your heart is on fire.

Show up. Fully. Loudly. Authentically.

Because the right people?

They won't ask you to tone it down.

They won't flinch at your truth.

They'll rise to meet your light—and reflect it right back.

You've made it this far. Through the ache, through the plot twists, through the chapters you never thought you'd survive.

And still, you're here. Still standing.

So today—choose you.

Choose truth.

Choose joy.

Choose healing that feels like home and love that feels like peace.

And let the rest catch up.

If you're in the middle of your unraveling, keep going.

If you're standing in front of a closed door, remember—you have your own keys.

If you've been written off, underestimated, counted out? Write yourself back in.

Because your story matters. Your voice matters. You matter.

Let my life be proof that no amount of loss can stop love. No amount of failure can kill purpose. And no amount of silence can drown out a voice that was born to speak truth.

Thank you for reading. For staying. For seeing me.

If no one's told you lately: *You are enough.*

Not when you lose the weight.

Not when you get the promotion.

Not when you fix what broke or finally stop crying.

You are enough *now*. In this mess. In this moment. In this becoming. Close the book if you must. But don't close the chapter on yourself.

Not yet.

You've still got pages left to write.

With love, light, and lessons learned,

Christopher Angel Machado

The End...

...of this story. But love? That's where the next one begins.

ACKNOWLEDGMENTS

To Julia and the late Antonio—you had already raised your own children, yet you opened your hearts and your home to a four-year-old boy who desperately needed stability, structure, and love. Antonio may no longer be with us, but his presence still echoes in the lessons he taught me, the strength he instilled in me, and the unwavering love he showed me. Julia, you never stopped choosing me—and together, you gave me the kind of selflessness and foundation that changed my life. I will forever be grateful to call you my parents in every way that matters.

To my family: There are not enough words on this page—nor within the chapters of this book—to fully express how deeply grateful I am for each of you. You've shown me what it means to love unconditionally, to lift each other through life's storms, and to pour into someone even when they fight you every step of the way. You are the living embodiment of "it takes a village to raise a child," and you've done it with grace, humor, and a whole lot of patience. This book is a testament to your sacrifices and love.

To Evelyn and Roberto—you made a promise to my mother on her deathbed to care for me after her passing. That wasn't just a moment; it became a lifetime commitment. For over three decades, you've kept that promise with unwavering devotion. You showed up for me in ways both big and small, and because of you, I never felt fully alone. You honored my mother's memory by loving her son like your own. I will never forget that.

To Madeline—Ours hasn't always been the easiest relationship—but what family ever is? Through the highs, the heartbreaks, the years we drifted and the moments we found our way back—you've always been a part of my foundation. You've taught me what it means to show up for the people you love, even when it's hard. Even when it hurts. And together, we've learned that healing doesn't always come in straight lines—but it comes, especially when we're willing to meet each other halfway. I hope this book reminds you that no matter the distance, time, or differences—we are forever connected.

To Junior—my brother—Life didn't always deal you the kindest hand, and after mom passed, the world pulled us in different directions. But no matter the miles or the years, you've always carried your own kind of strength—the quiet, steady kind. You're the proud father of two beautiful kids, Haley and Junior, and the way you love and show up for them? It inspires me. You work hard to give them the life and chances we didn't always have—and I aspire to be the kind of father you are. This book is a testament to resilience, and you're part of that story. Thank you for being in mine.

To Sandra—Thank you for being the sister I chose and the steady hand I didn't know I needed. You loved me through every high, every heartbreak, and every silent moment in between—without judgment, without conditions, and without ever letting go. You made space for my healing and carried parts of my story with more care than I could have ever asked for. I am who I am, in part, because you stayed. I will spend a lifetime grateful for you. You didn't just stay—you made sure I never had to walk alone. And for that, I am endlessly thankful.

To Reina (Lucas) Murray—my high school guidance counselor turned lifelong friend—thank you for having the patience to meet me where I was and the wisdom to guide me where I needed to go. You saw something in me I didn't yet know existed. You believed in me at a time when I barely believed in myself. I carry your impact with me always.

To my best friends: Thank you for being my chosen family—the ones who accept me at my most unfiltered, who laugh with me, cry with me, and hold space for me just as I am.

To Cassie—thank you for saving my life and standing by me for over 22 years. Through every season, every heartbreak, and every triumph, you never wavered. I am forever grateful for you.

To Perla—my soul-sister—thank you for being my ride-or-die, my co-conspirator in chaos, my soft place to land, and the one who simply gets me. What we have is more than friendship—it's soul-deep, storm-tested, and impossibly rare.

To Jimmy—my neighbor turned chosen family—thank you for being the gay Puerto Rican uncle I didn't know I needed. Your warmth, humor, and wisdom have been a constant light in my life. Thank you for every late-night talk, every plate of food you shared with me, and for loving Milo like your own. You reminded me that community isn't just about who lives next door—it's about who shows up with open arms and good advice when life gets heavy. I'm endlessly grateful for your care, your kindness, and the way you always know exactly what to say. You've been both a soft place to land and a gentle push forward—and for that, I'll always be thankful.

To Terry—my roommate turned close friend and confidant—thank you for being my sounding board through every chapter, every rewrite, every moment of self-doubt. I'm truly grateful for your friendship—and for always reminding me that our stories deserve to be told with authenticity.

To my mentors and work friends: Thank you for guiding me, challenging me, and pouring into me professionally and personally. Whether it was a word of encouragement during a hard day, advice that shaped my career, or just a shared laugh in the chaos of the workroom—you made all the difference. You reminded me that leadership isn't about a title—it's about impact, heart, and courage. Thank you for helping me find mine.

To my teachers—inside and outside the classroom: Thank you for seeing me before I ever saw myself. You didn't just teach me subjects—you taught me to think, to question, to hope, and to heal. Your lessons reached far beyond the classroom, shaping my heart and my future in ways a curriculum never could. You taught me that every story matters, and you gave me the courage to tell mine. This book—and the person I've become—exists because you believed I could rise.

To my haters, the cynics, and the skeptics: Thank you for purchasing this book. Your doubt fed my fire, your shade grew my success, and I rose from the ashes you lit for me. Thanks for the motivation.

Finally, in the immortal words of the iconic Niecy Nash-Betts: *"You know who I wanna thank? I want to thank me, for believing in me and for doing what they said I could not do. Go, girl, with your bad self. You did that!"*

A NOTE FROM THE AUTHOR

If this story moved you, I hope you'll consider sharing it—with someone you love, someone who's hurting, or someone who might just need a reminder that they're not alone.

Memoirs are intimate by nature, but they're not meant to live in isolation. They're meant to start conversations. To break silence. To reach across the distance between us and say, *"Me too."*

So if you found something in these pages—be it comfort, courage, clarity, or even just the feeling of being seen—I invite you to pass that feeling forward. Recommend it to a friend. Lend it to a loved one. Screenshot a quote that resonated and post it. Because sometimes, the right words land at exactly the right moment.

I also ask, with deep humility, that you consider leaving a review online. Not just for me—but for the next reader standing in the bookstore aisle (or scrolling Amazon at 2 a.m.) who's trying to decide if this is the story they need. Your voice helps this story travel farther than I ever could on my own.

And if you want to talk more—about writing, healing, heartbreak, or what it means to piece together a new life after loss—I'd love to connect. You can find me here:

- **Instagram:** @TheOfficialChristopherMachado
- **X (Twitter):** @IamChrisMachado
- **Facebook:** www.facebook.com/machado.christopher
- **LinkedIn:** www.linkedin.com/in/christopheramachado

Until then, stay standing. Stay soft. Stay bold.

With love and gratitude,

Christopher Angel Machado

The Faces Behind the Pages

Before the world tried to rewrite me, they wrote the first draft.

These are the faces that built my foundation — my parents, and
the boy who learned from their love. Before the heartbreak,
before the healing, there was this: family, faith, and a kind of love
that never really leaves. These pages may tell the story, but these
pictures show the reason I'm still standing.

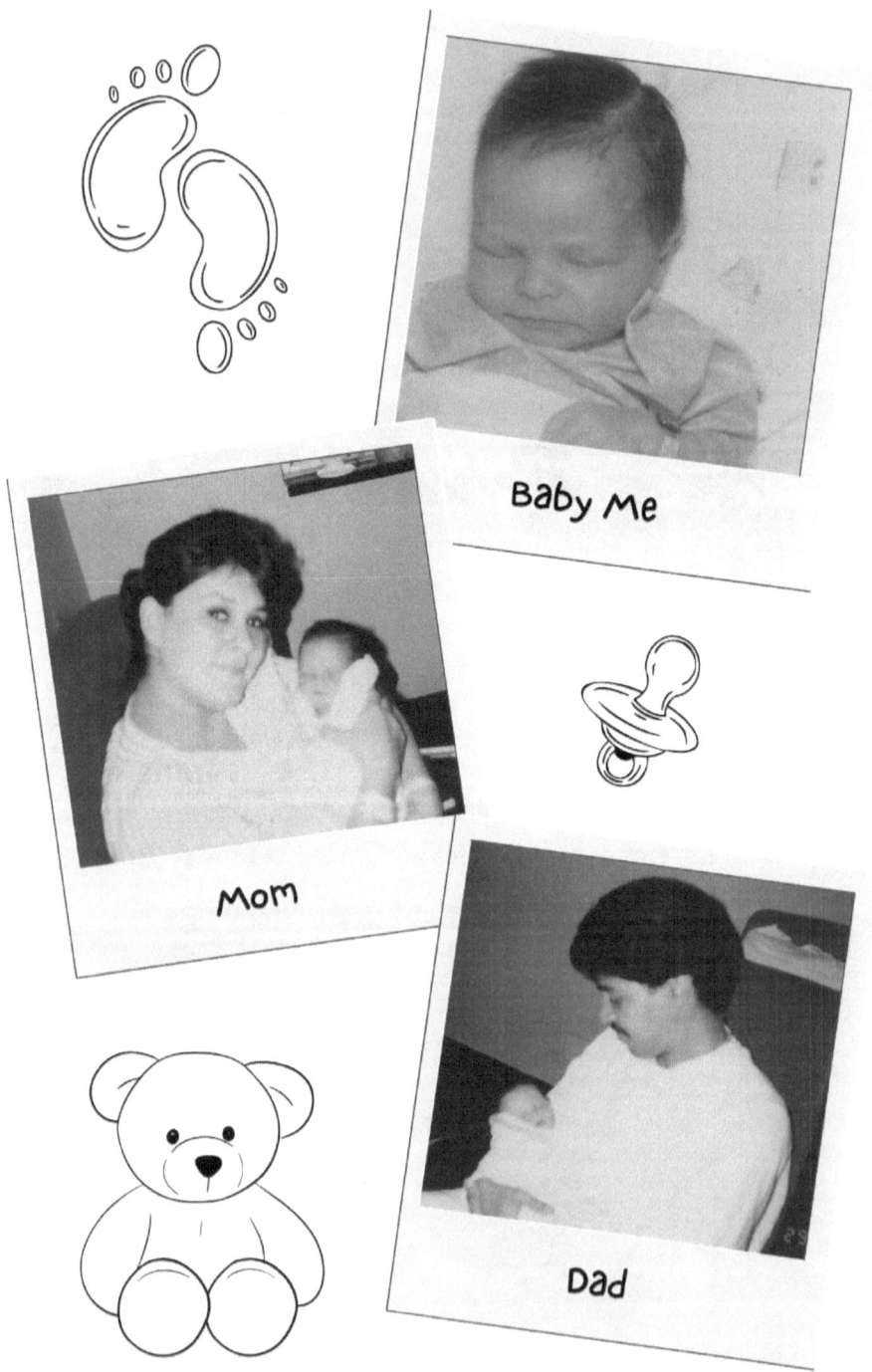

Baby Me

Mom

Dad

XOXO

love

family

OUR family

I LOVE YOU

memories

family
is
EVERYTHING

DAD

Big Bro

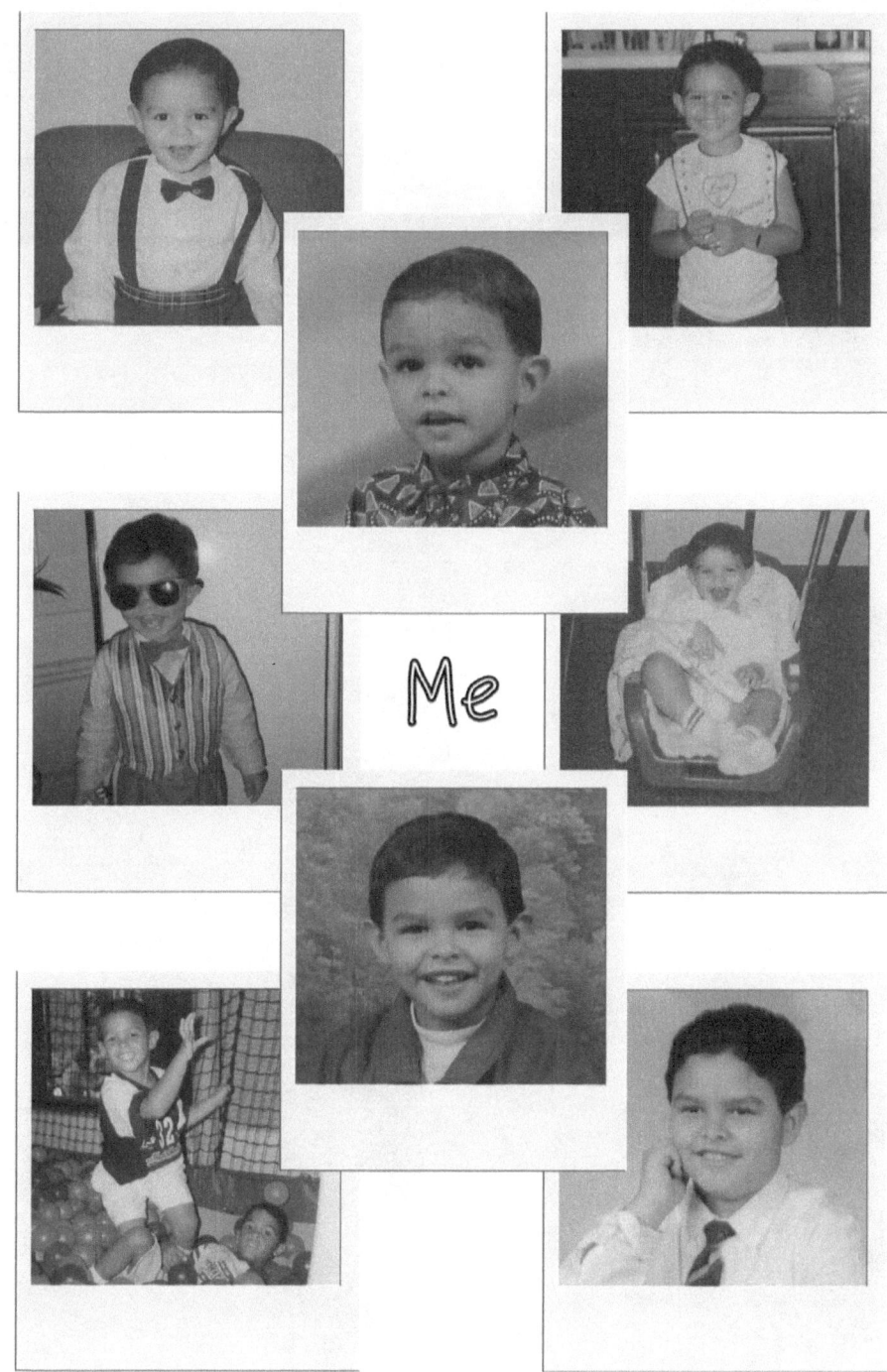

Me

STILL I STAND:
A LIFE REWRITTEN

Thank You

Christopher Angel Machado, M.Ed.

www.ingramcontent.com/pod-product-compliance
Lightning Source LLC
Chambersburg PA
CBHW030916120626
46554CB00001B/173